MARVEL SUPER HERO SQUAD

SQUAD UP!

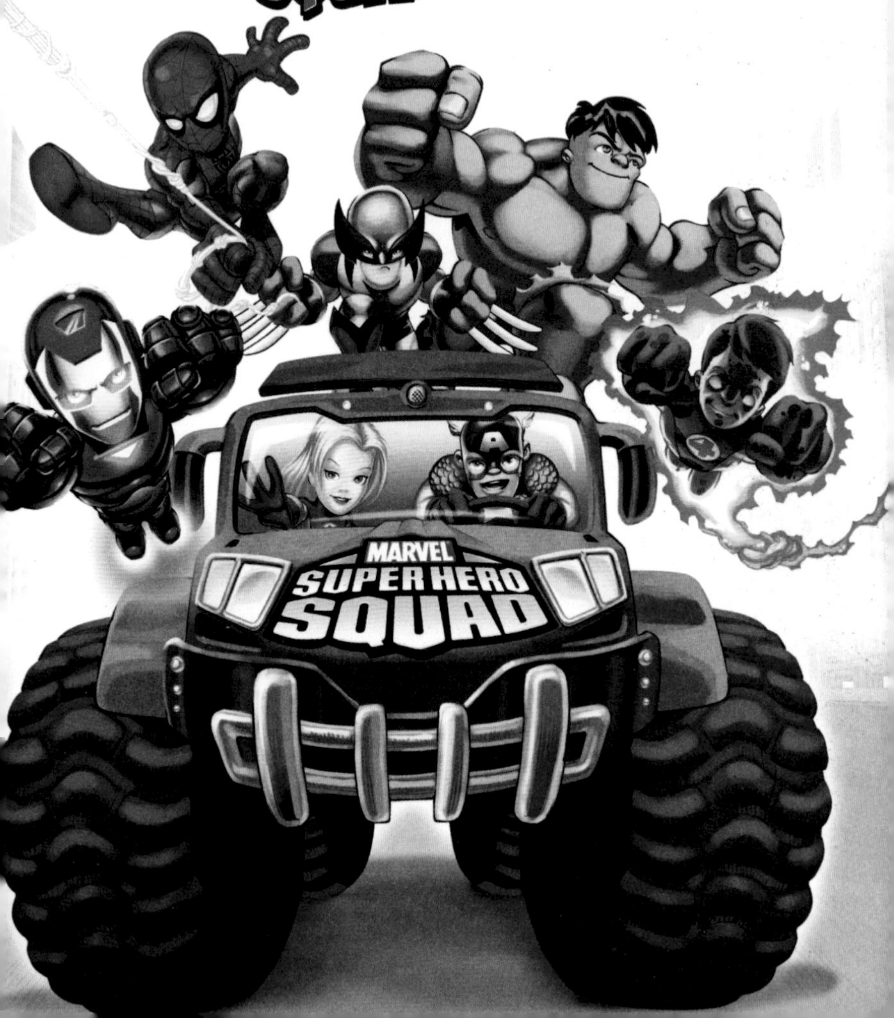
MARVEL
SUPER HERO
SQUAD

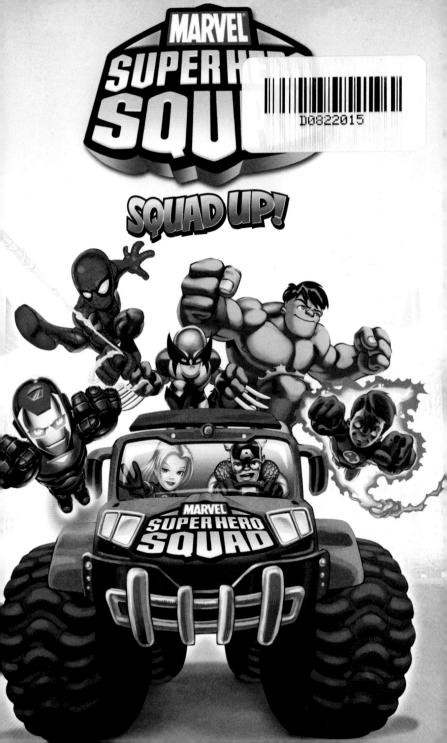

MARVEL SUPER HERO SQUAD

SQUAD UP!

WRITER: PAUL TOBIN

ARTIST: DARIO BRIZUELA

LETTERER: DAVE SHARPE

ASSISTANT EDITOR: MICHAEL HORWITZ

EDITOR: NATHAN COSBY

SPECIAL THANKS TO COURTNEY LANE, KAT JONES, CHRIS FONDACARO & TOM MARVELLI

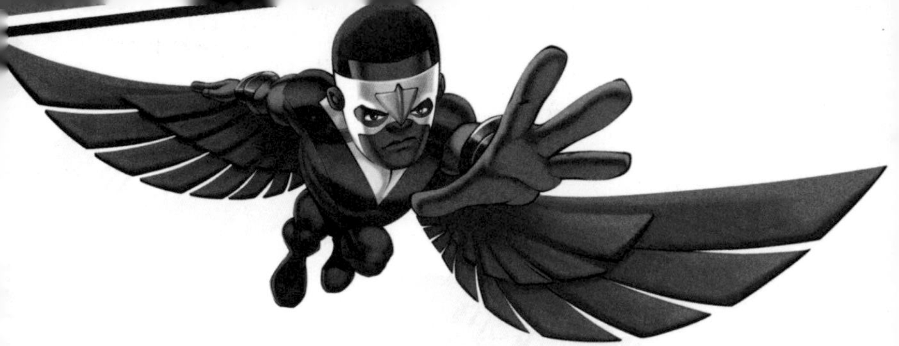

COLLECTION EDITOR: CORY LEVINE
EDITORIAL ASSISTANTS: JAMES EMMETT & JOE HOCHSTEIN
ASSISTANT EDITORS: ALEX STARBUCK & NELSON RIBEIRO
EDITORS, SPECIAL PROJECTS: JENNIFER GRÜNWALD & MARK D. BEAZLEY
SENIOR EDITOR, SPECIAL PROJECTS: JEFF YOUNGQUIST
SENIOR VICE PRESIDENT OF SALES: DAVID GABRIEL
BOOK DESIGN: PATRICK McGRATH

EDITOR IN CHIEF: JOE QUESADA
PUBLISHER: DAN BUCKLEY
EXECUTIVE PRODUCER: ALAN FINE

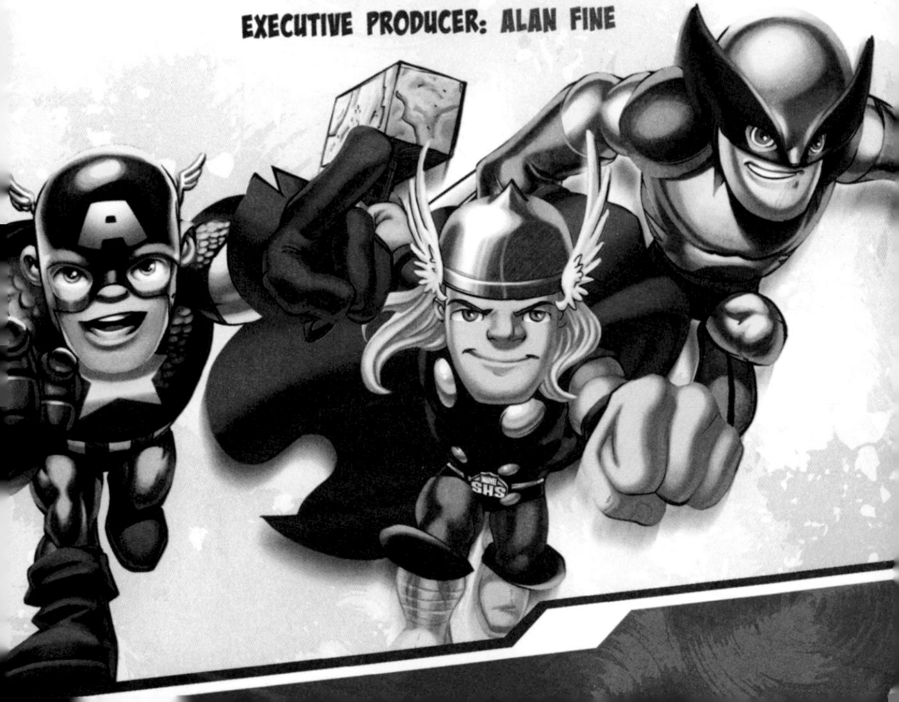

SHS

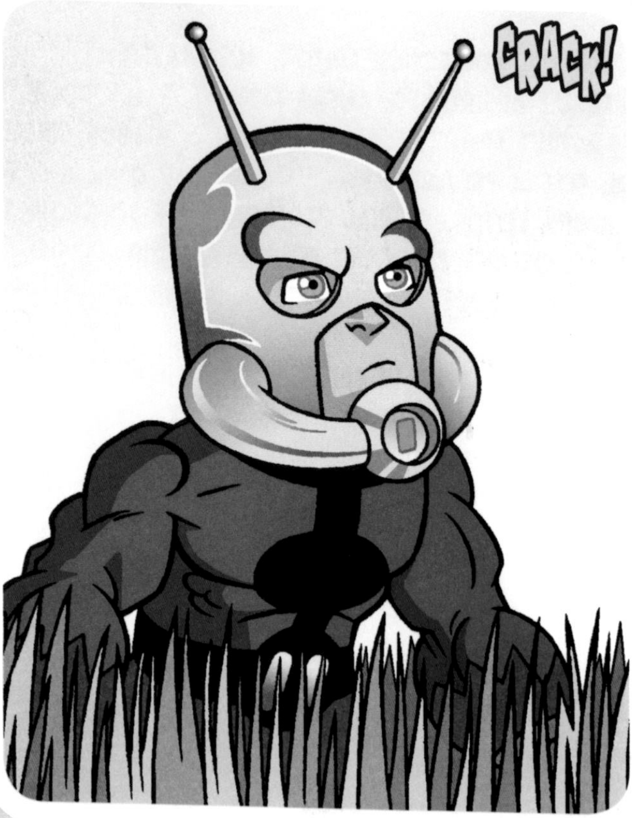
CRACK!

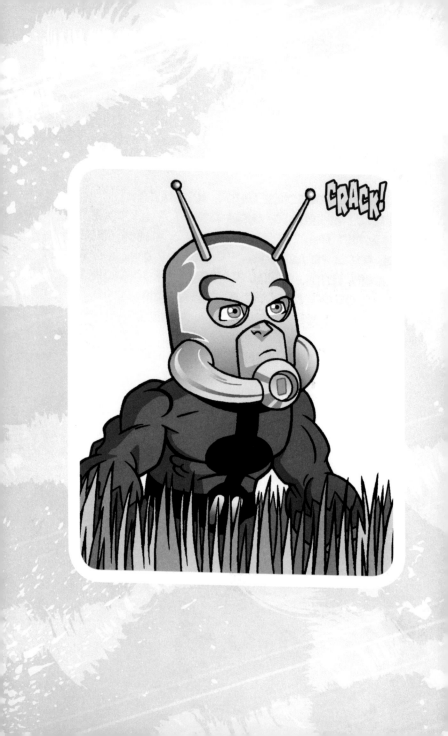

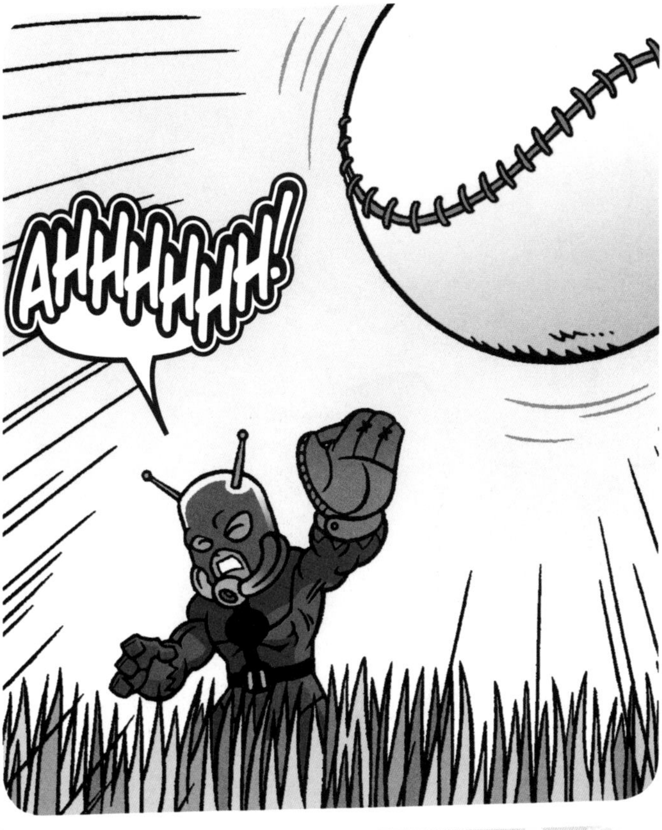
AHHHHHH!

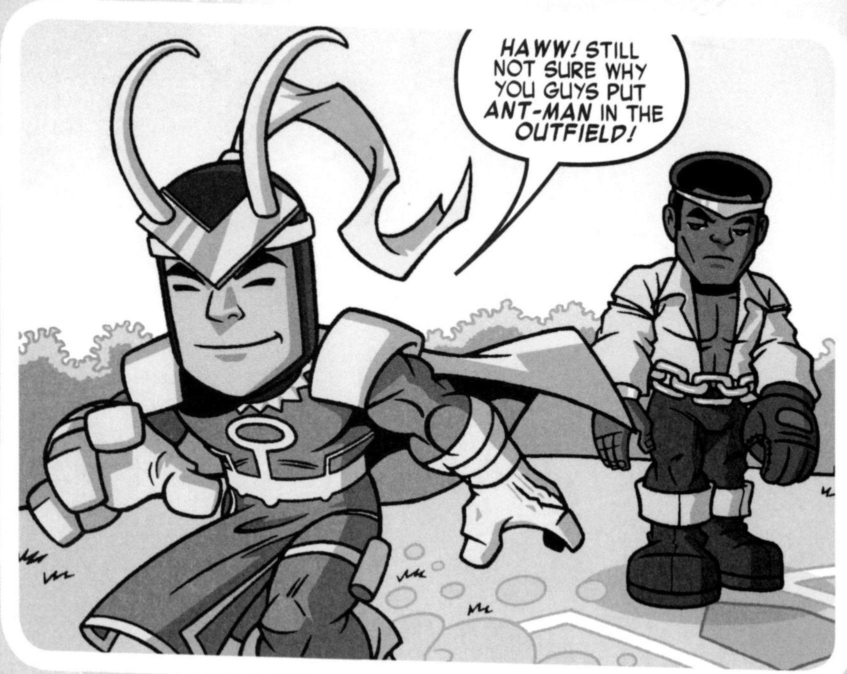
HAWW! STILL NOT SURE WHY YOU GUYS PUT ANT-MAN IN THE OUTFIELD!

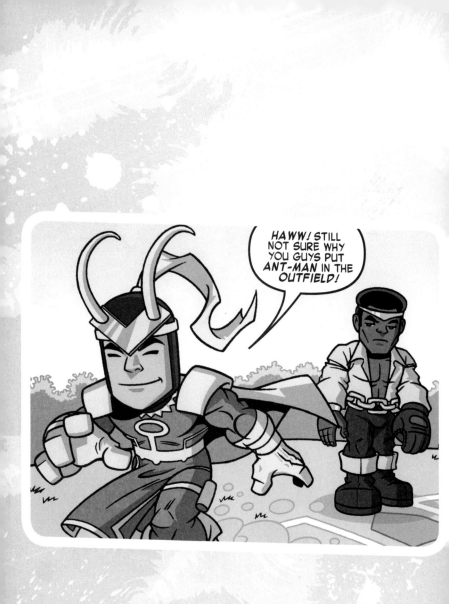

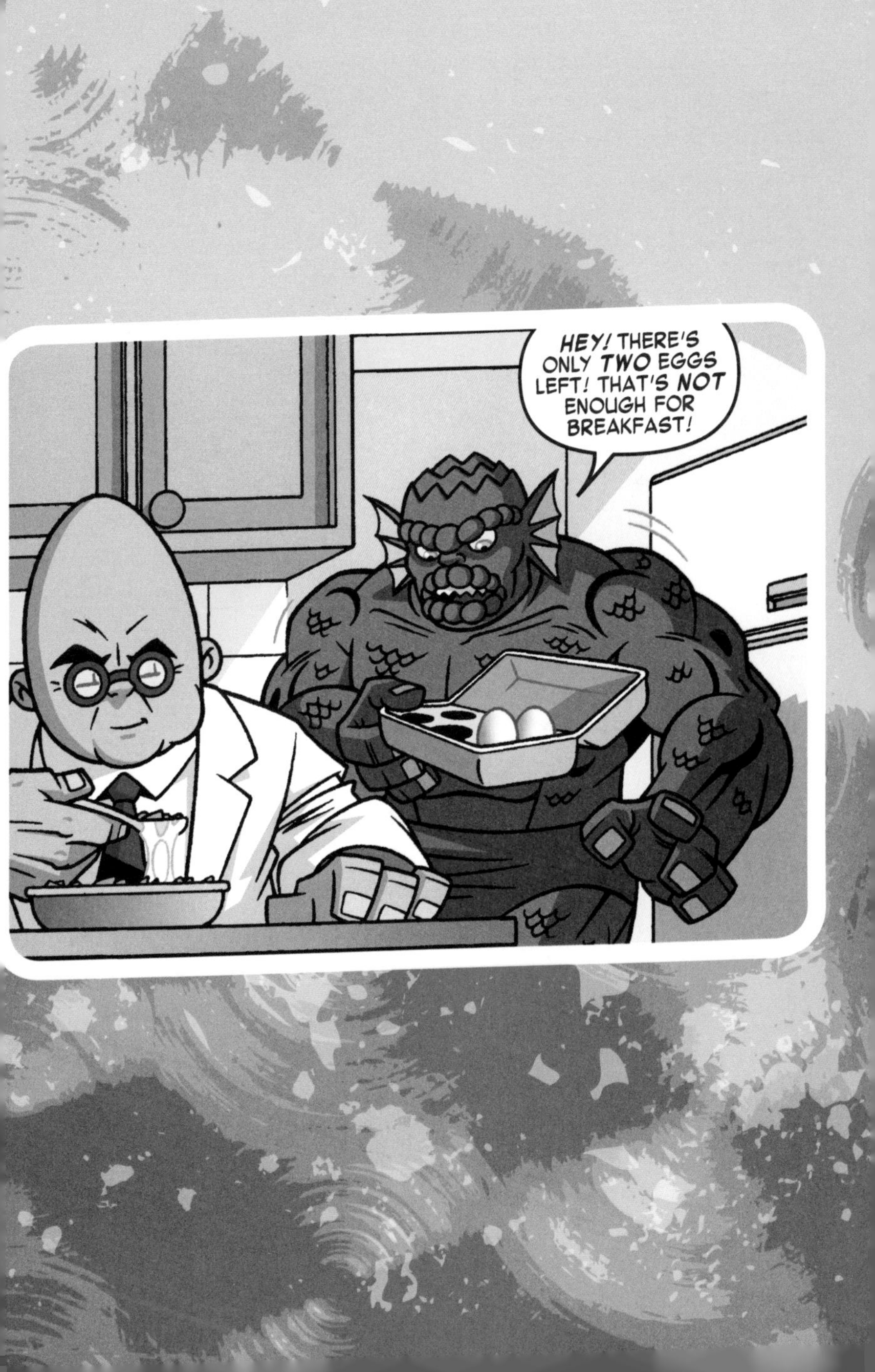
HEY! THERE'S ONLY TWO EGGS LEFT! THAT'S NOT ENOUGH FOR BREAKFAST!

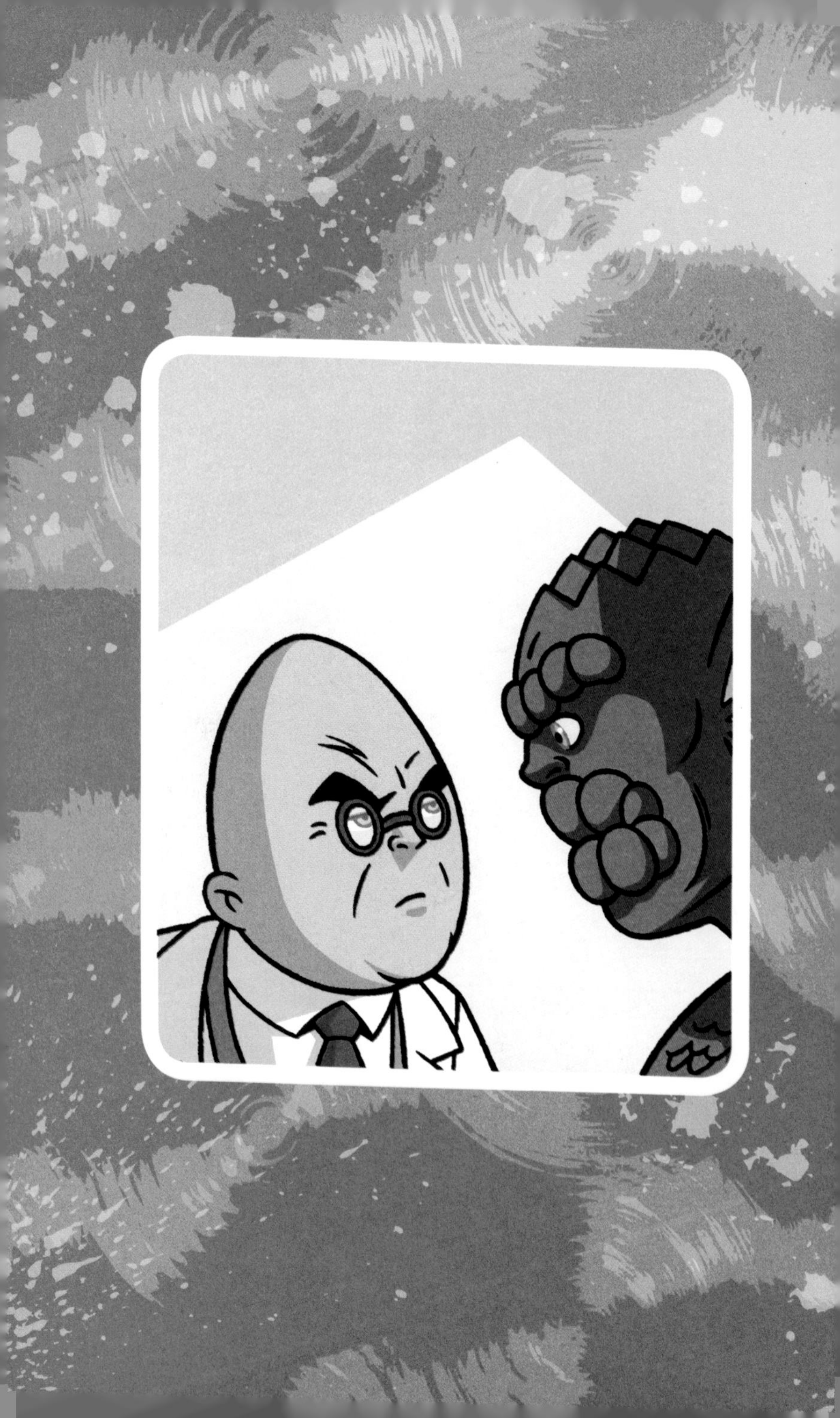

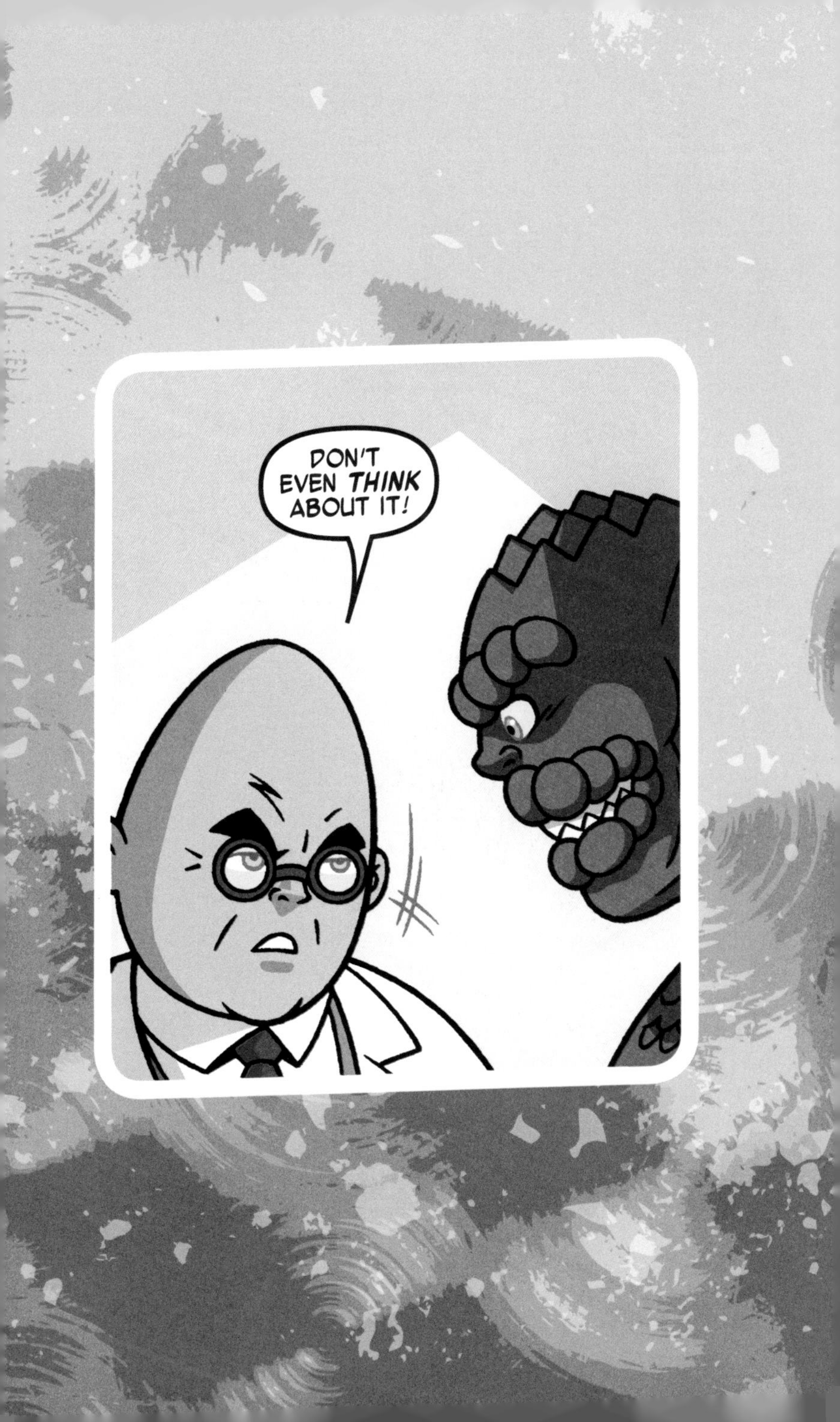
DON'T EVEN *THINK* ABOUT IT!

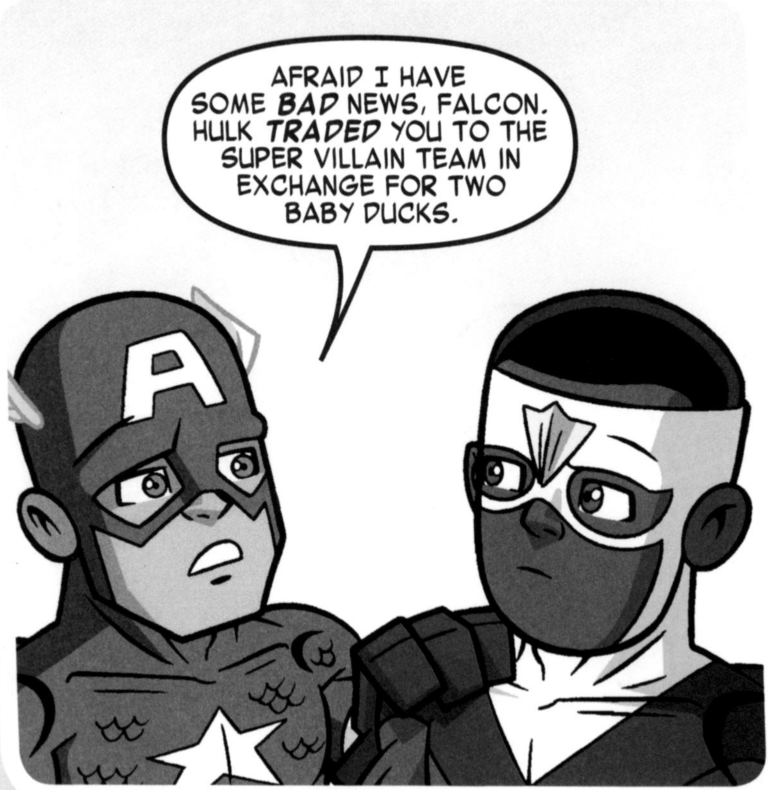
AFRAID I HAVE SOME BAD NEWS, FALCON. HULK TRADED YOU TO THE SUPER VILLAIN TEAM IN EXCHANGE FOR TWO BABY DUCKS.

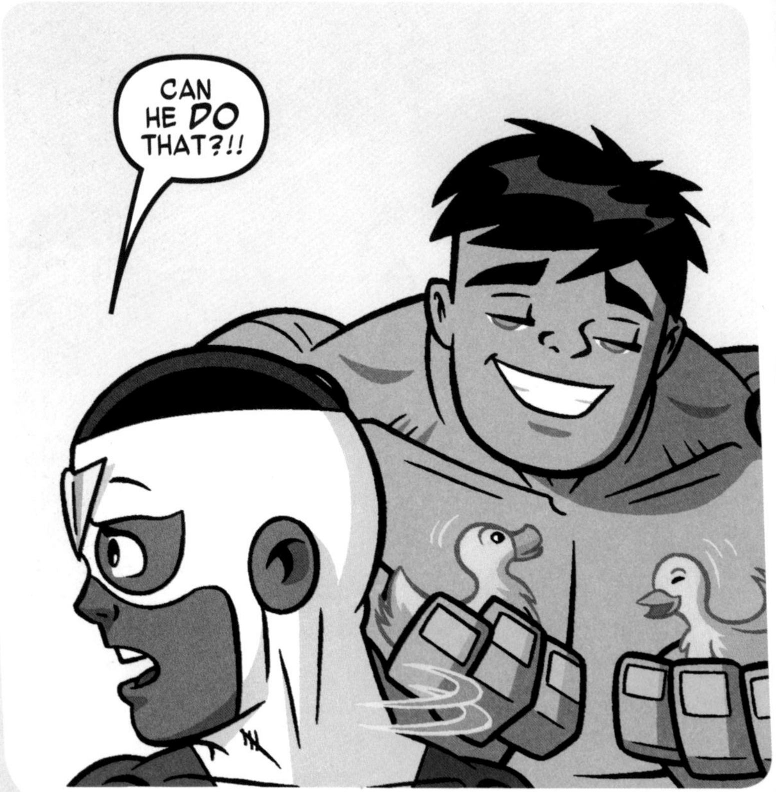
CAN HE DO THAT?!!

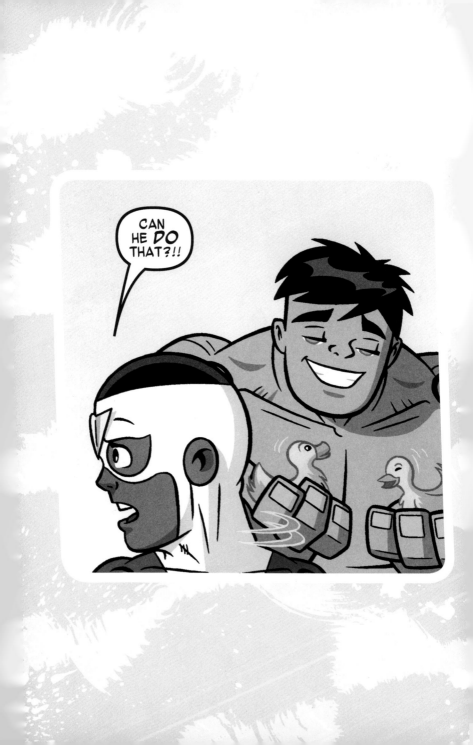

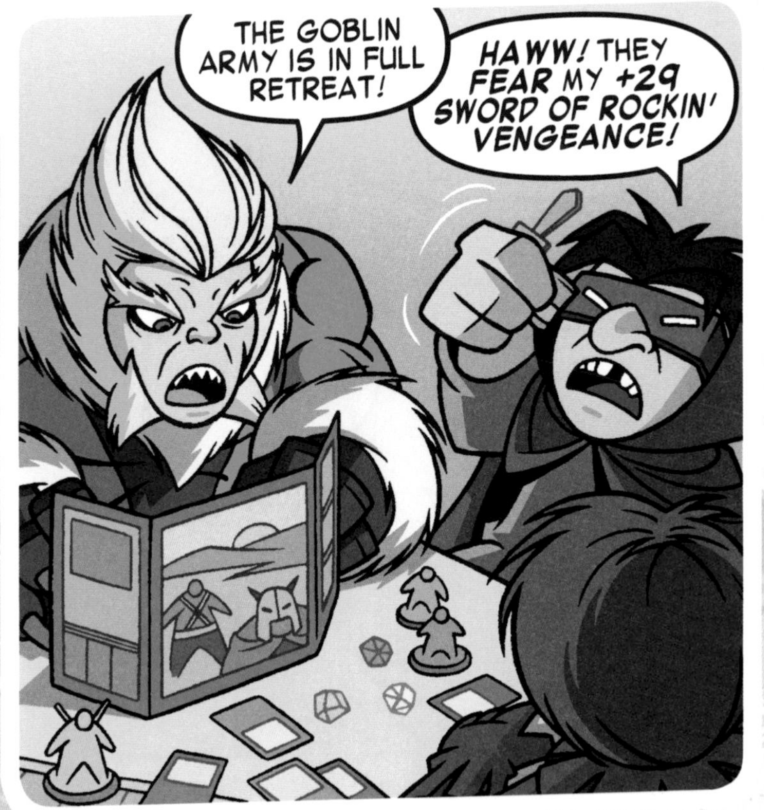
THE GOBLIN ARMY IS IN FULL RETREAT!
HAWW! THEY FEAR MY +29 SWORD OF ROCKIN' VENGEANCE!

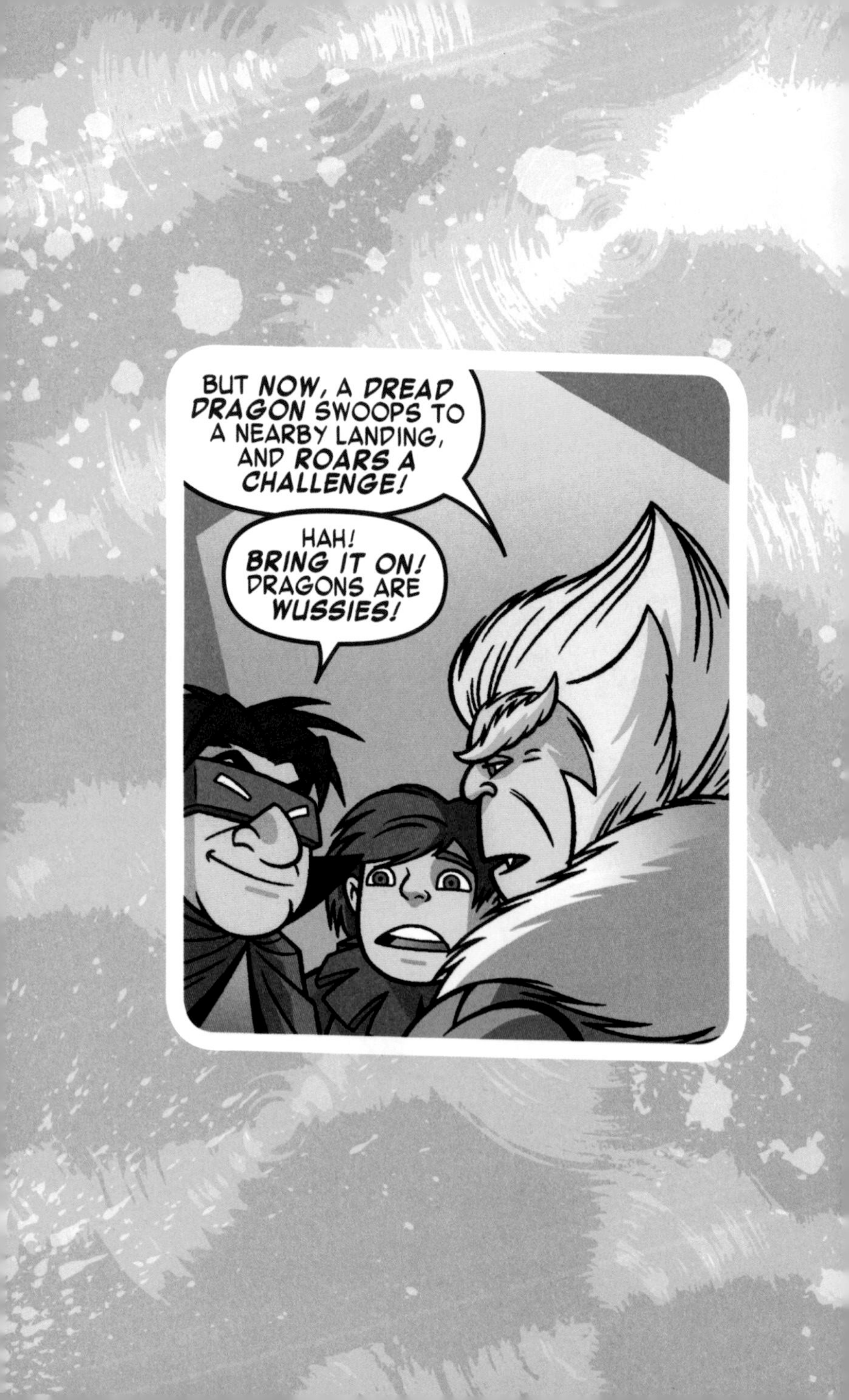
BUT NOW, A DREAD DRAGON SWOOPS TO A NEARBY LANDING, AND ROARS A CHALLENGE!
HAH! BRING IT ON! DRAGONS ARE WUSSIES!

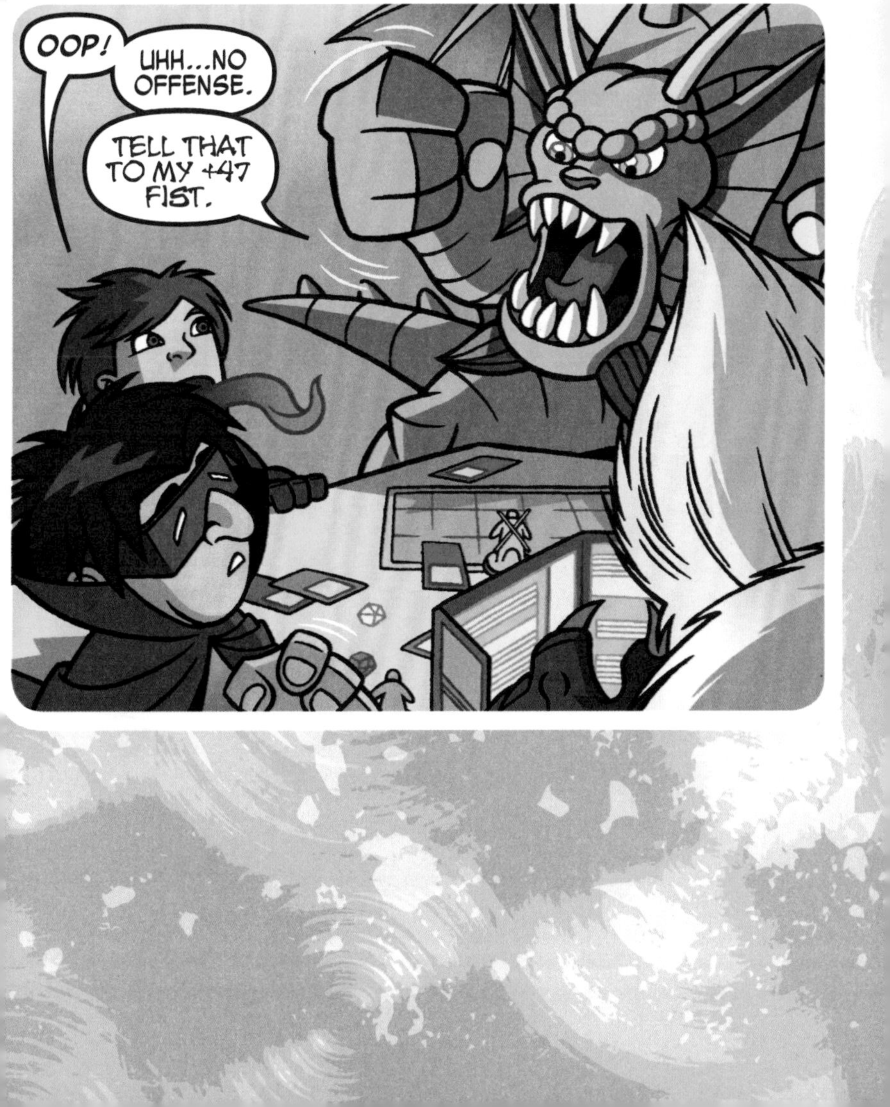
OOP!
UHH...NO OFFENSE.
TELL THAT TO MY +47 FIST.

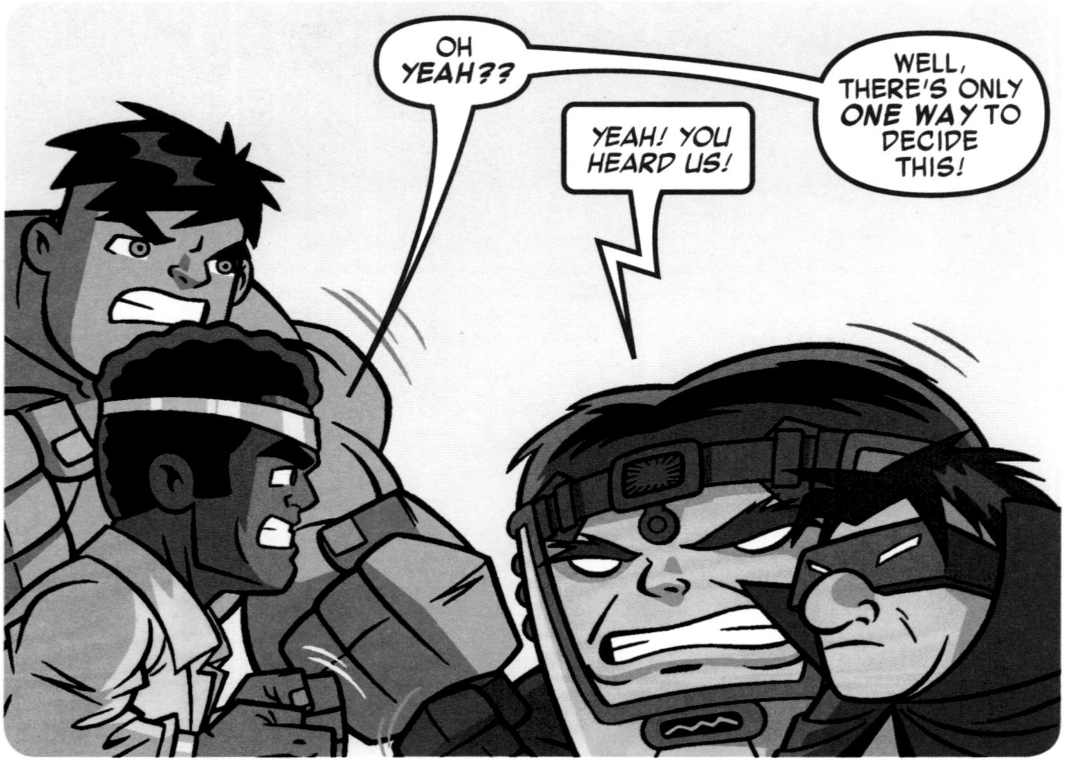
OH *YEAH??*
YEAH! YOU HEARD US!
WELL, THERE'S ONLY *ONE WAY* TO DECIDE THIS!

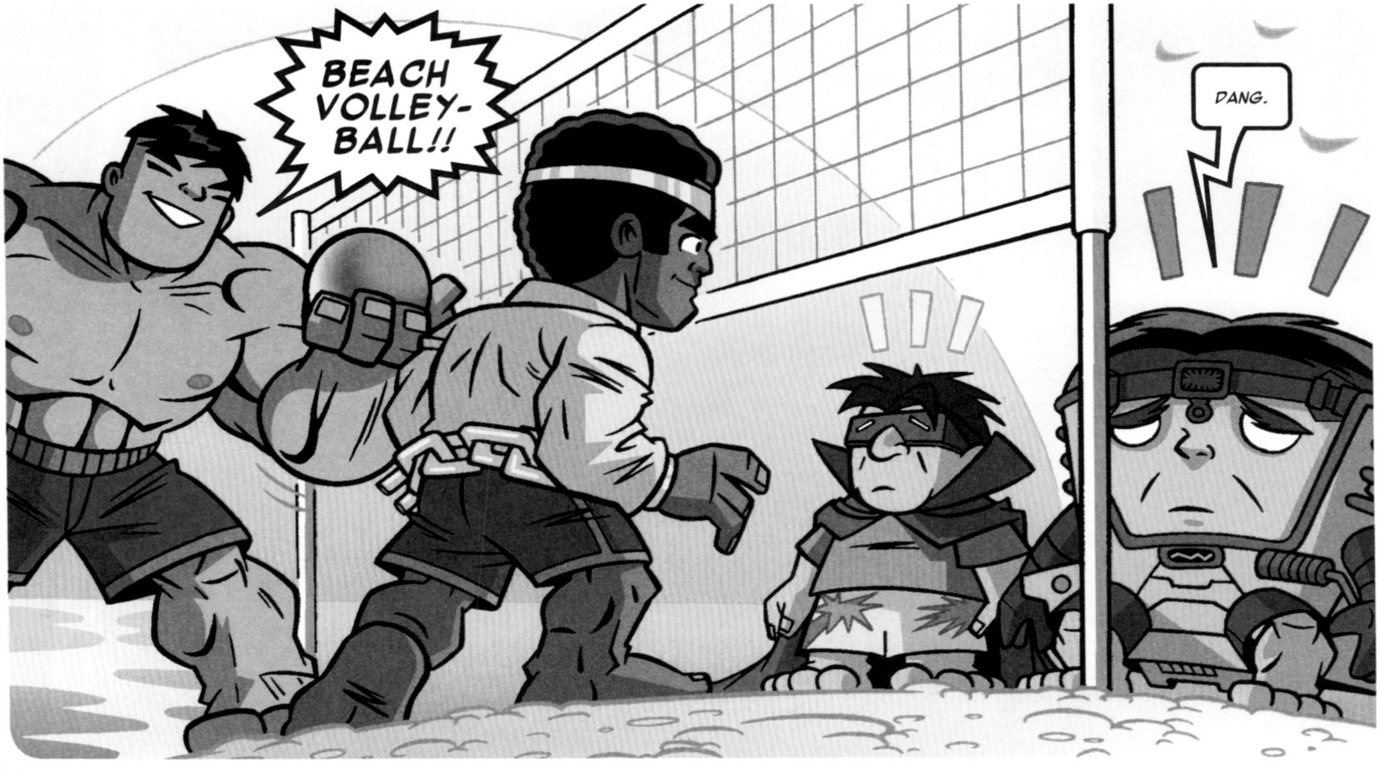
BEACH VOLLEY-BALL!!
DANG.

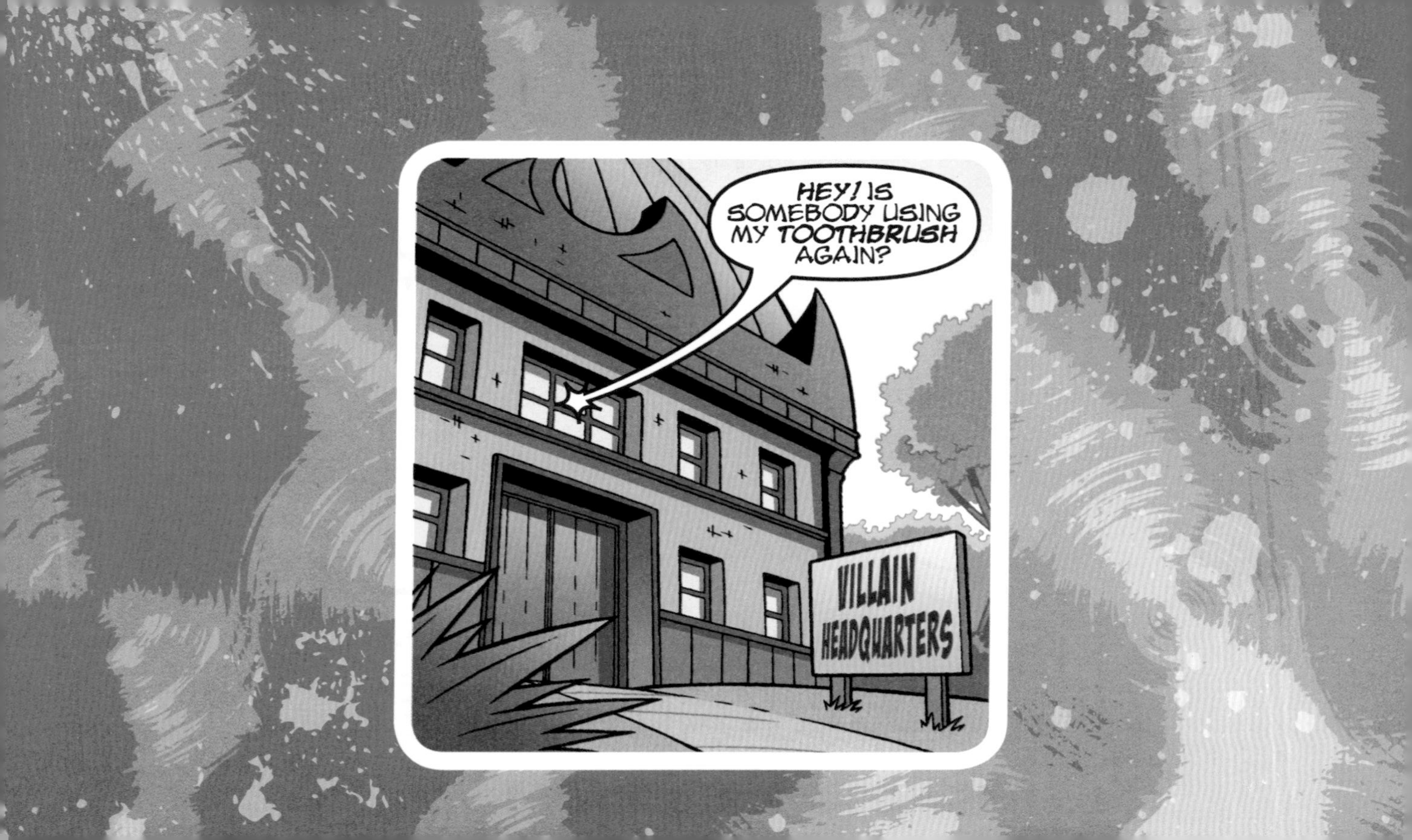
HEY! IS SOMEBODY USING MY TOOTHBRUSH AGAIN?
VILLAIN HEADQUARTERS

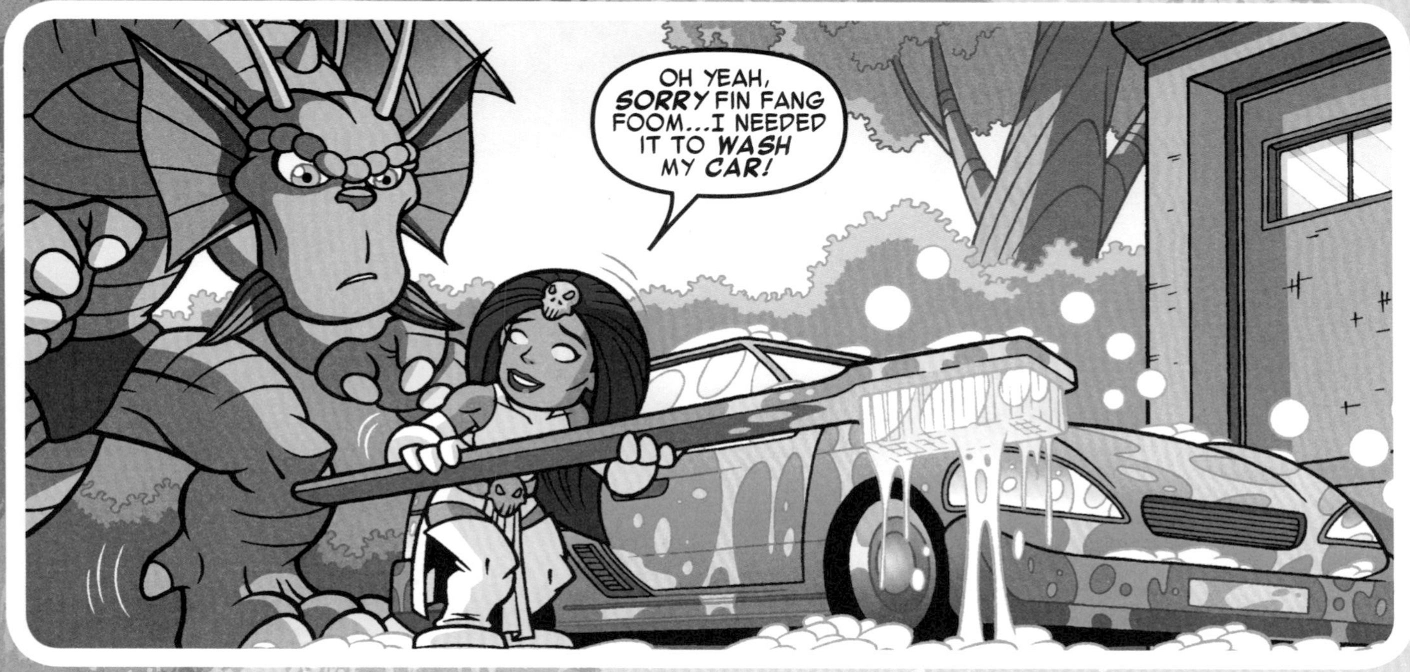
OH YEAH, SORRY FIN FANG FOOM...I NEEDED IT TO WASH MY CAR!

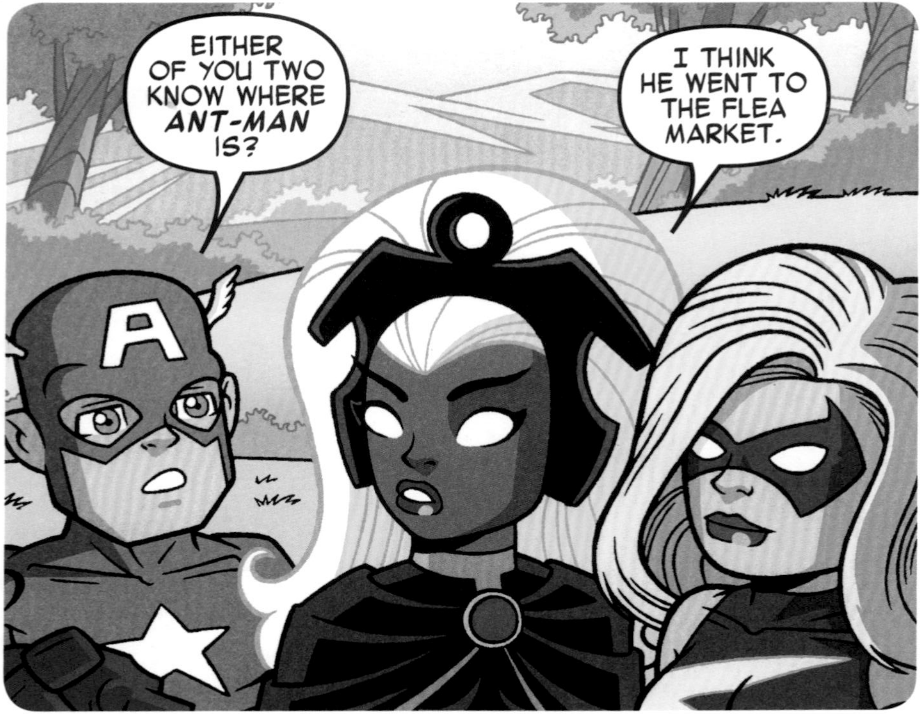

EITHER OF YOU TWO KNOW WHERE *ANT-MAN* IS?
I THINK HE WENT TO THE FLEA MARKET.

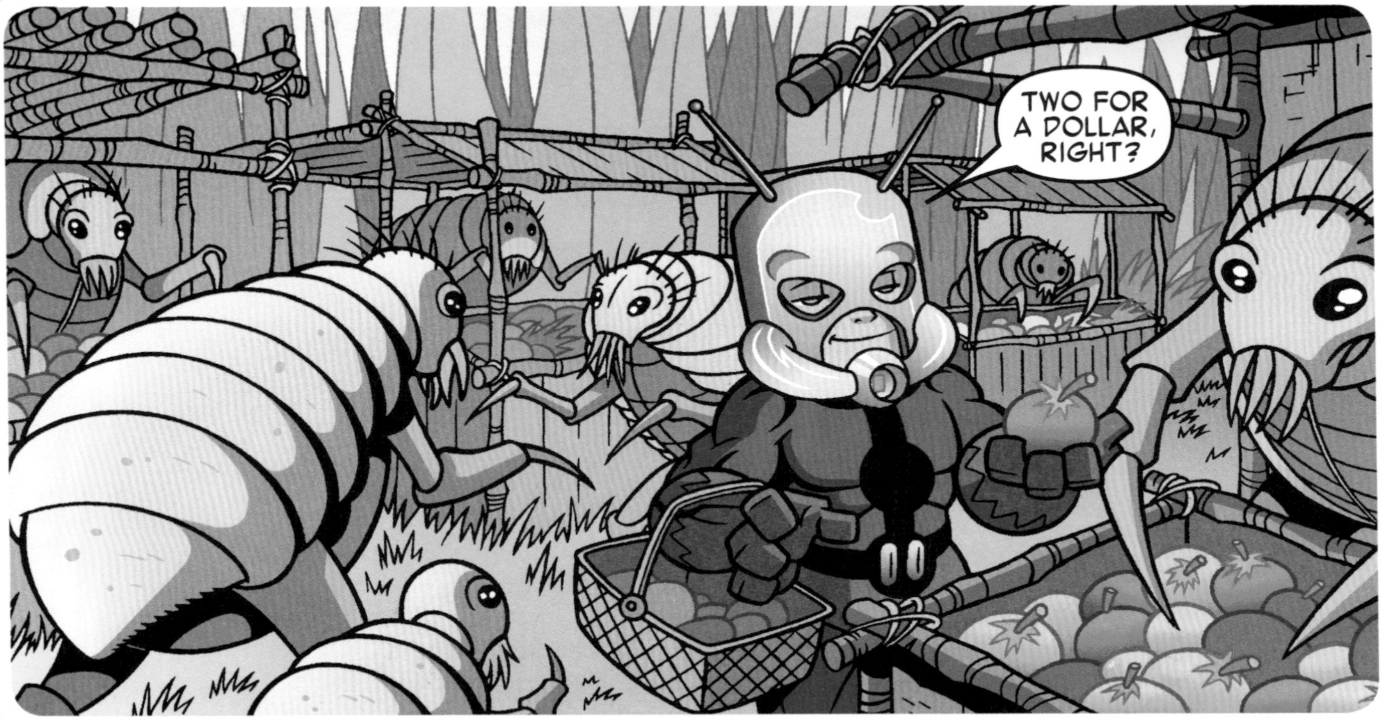
TWO FOR A DOLLAR, RIGHT?

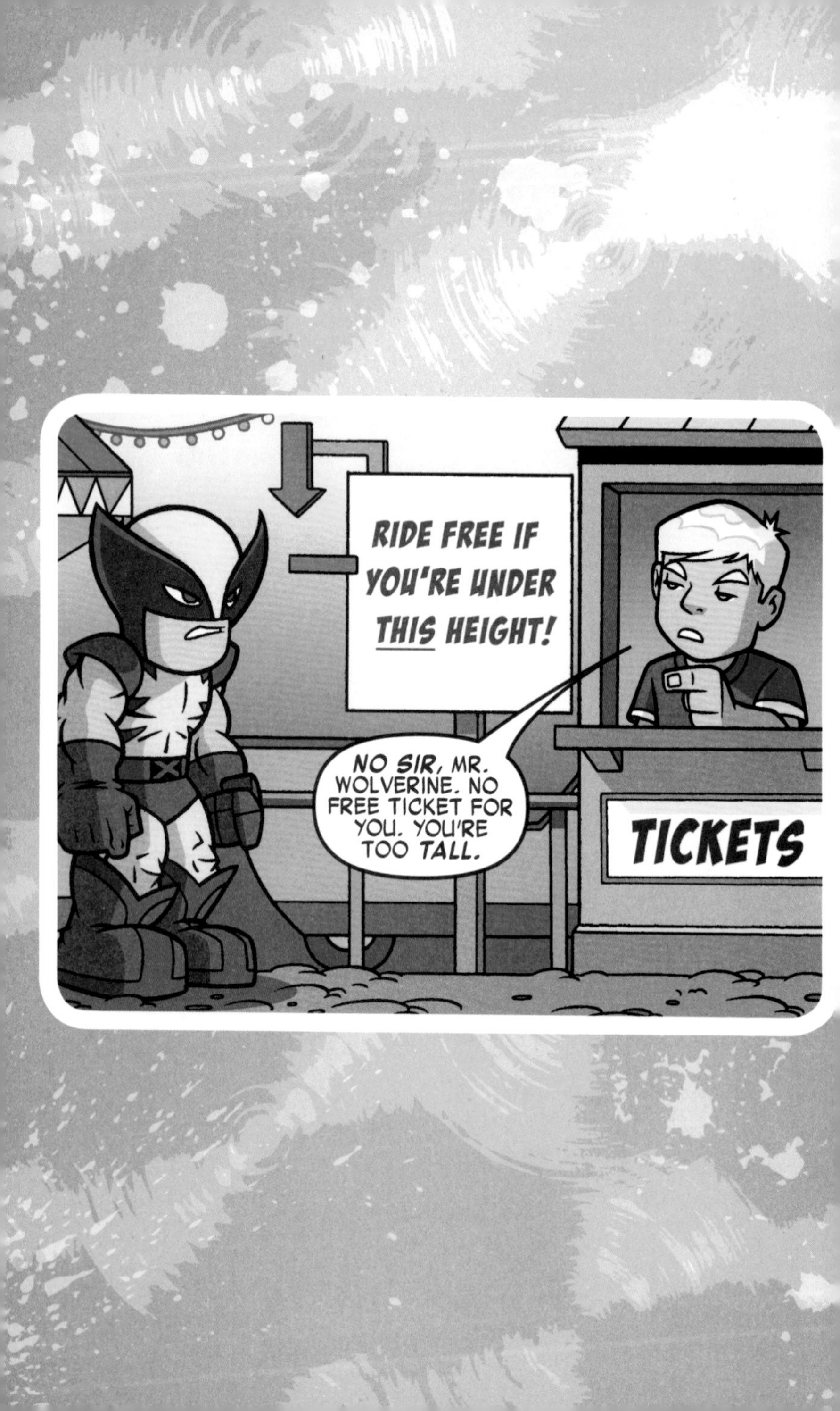
RIDE FREE IF YOU'RE UNDER THIS HEIGHT!
NO SIR, MR. WOLVERINE. NO FREE TICKET FOR YOU. YOU'RE TOO TALL.
TICKETS

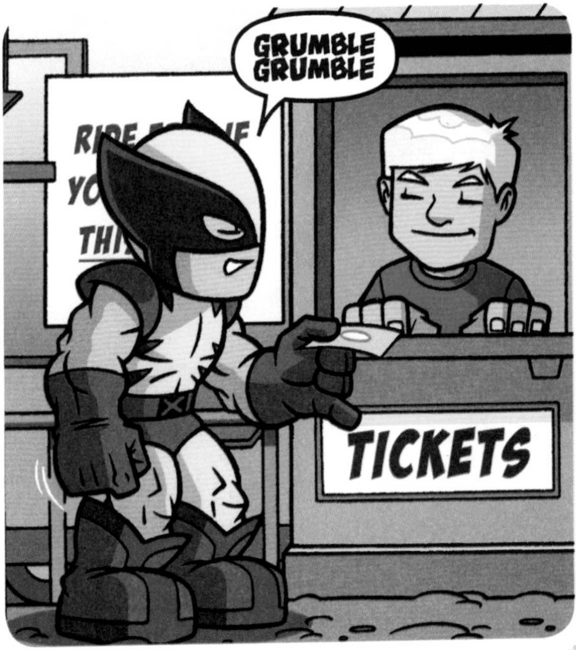
GRUMBLE GRUMBLE
TICKETS

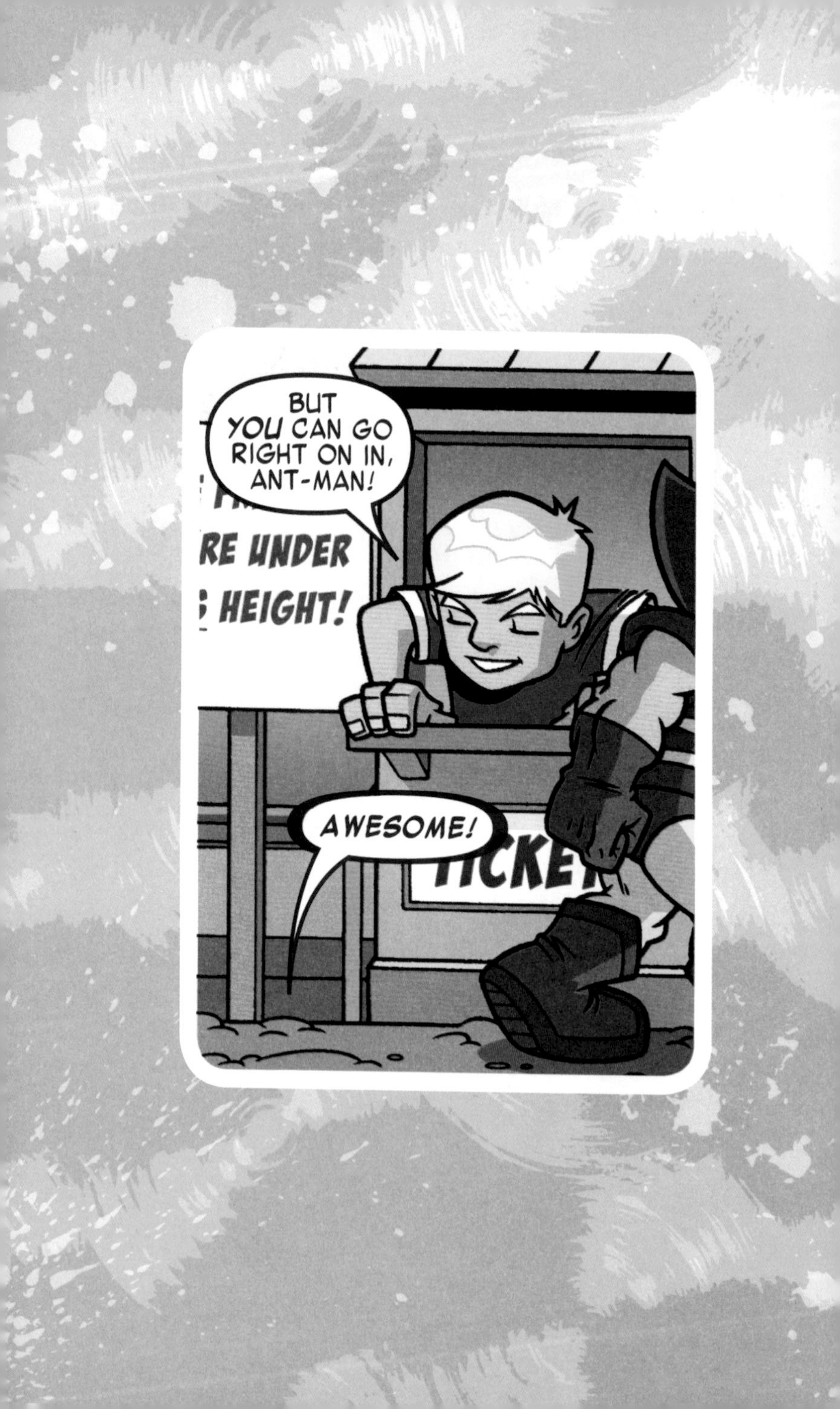

BUT YOU CAN GO RIGHT ON IN, ANT-MAN!
RE UNDER
HEIGHT!
AWESOME!

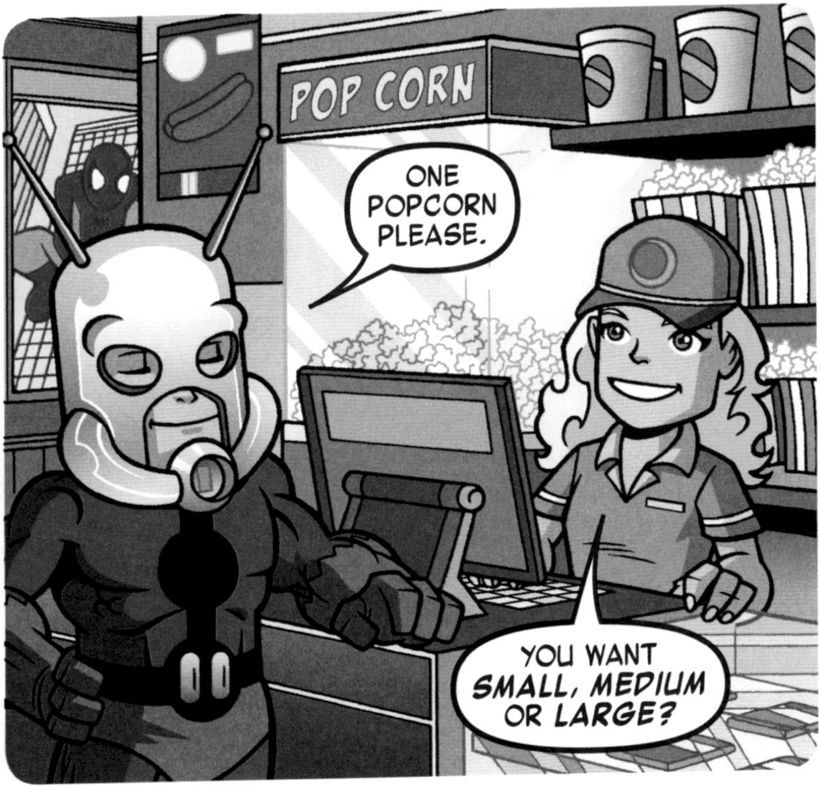
POP CORN
ONE POPCORN PLEASE.
YOU WANT SMALL, MEDIUM OR LARGE?

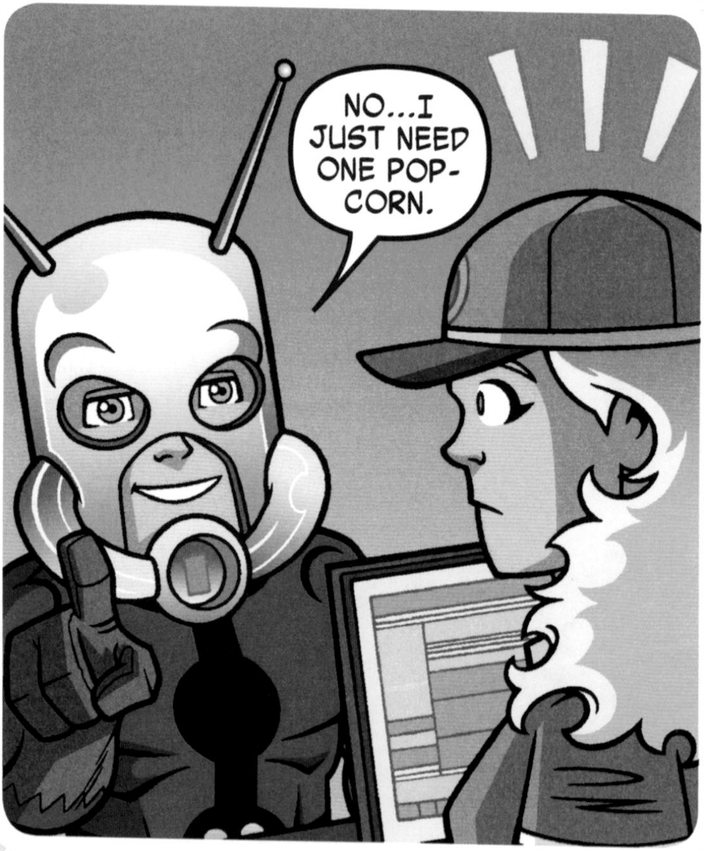
NO...I JUST NEED ONE POP-CORN.

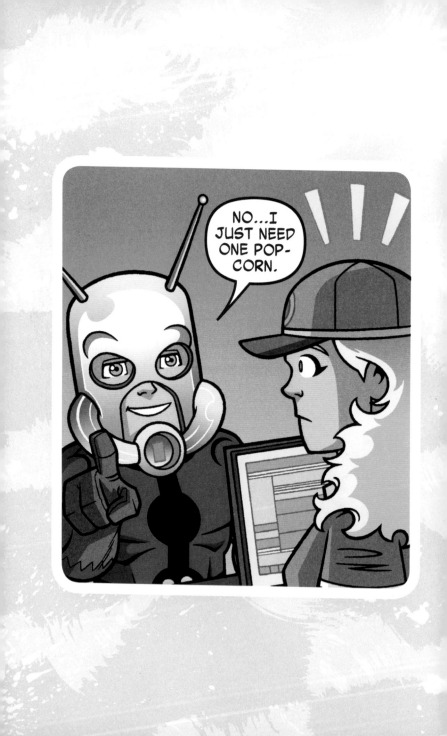

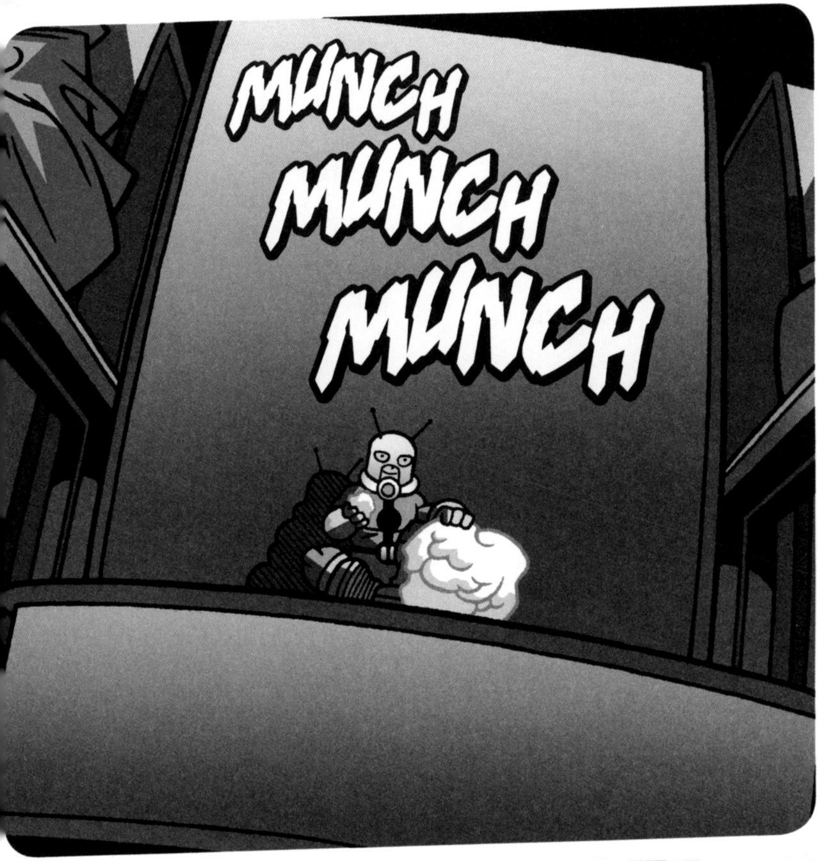
MUNCH
MUNCH
MUNCH

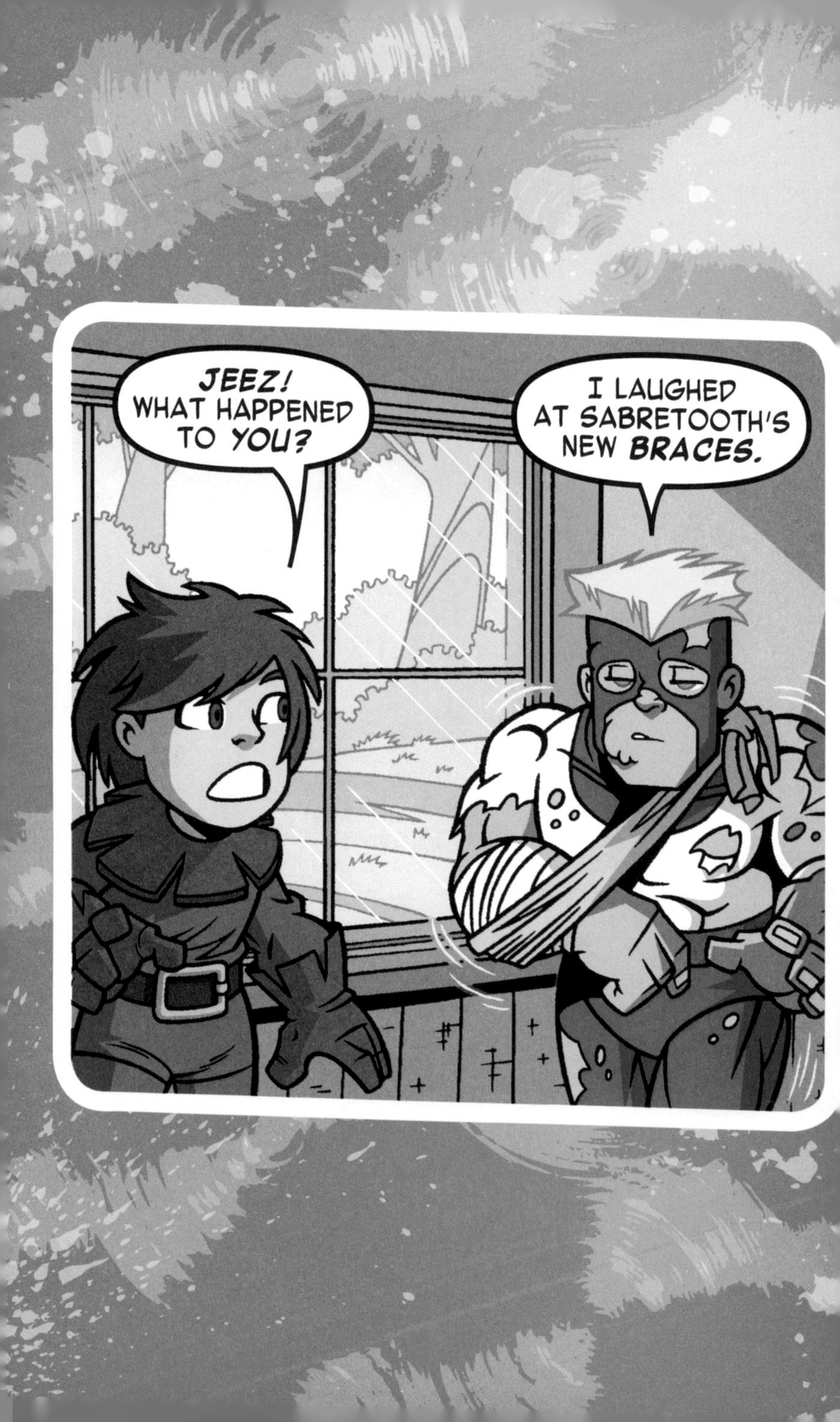
JEEZ! WHAT HAPPENED TO YOU?
I LAUGHED AT SABRETOOTH'S NEW BRACES.

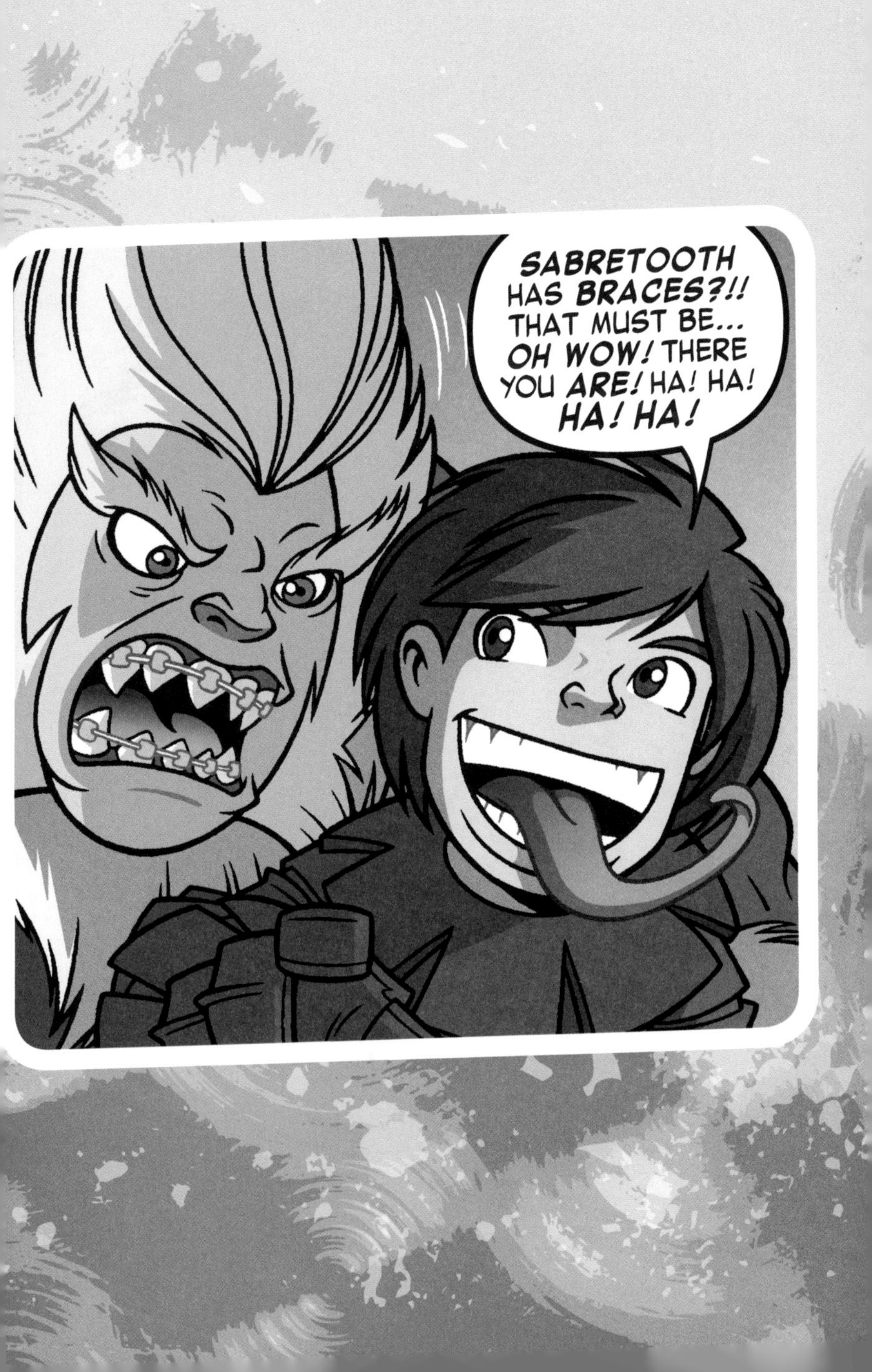
SABRETOOTH HAS BRACES?!! THAT MUST BE... OH WOW! THERE YOU ARE! HA! HA! HA! HA!

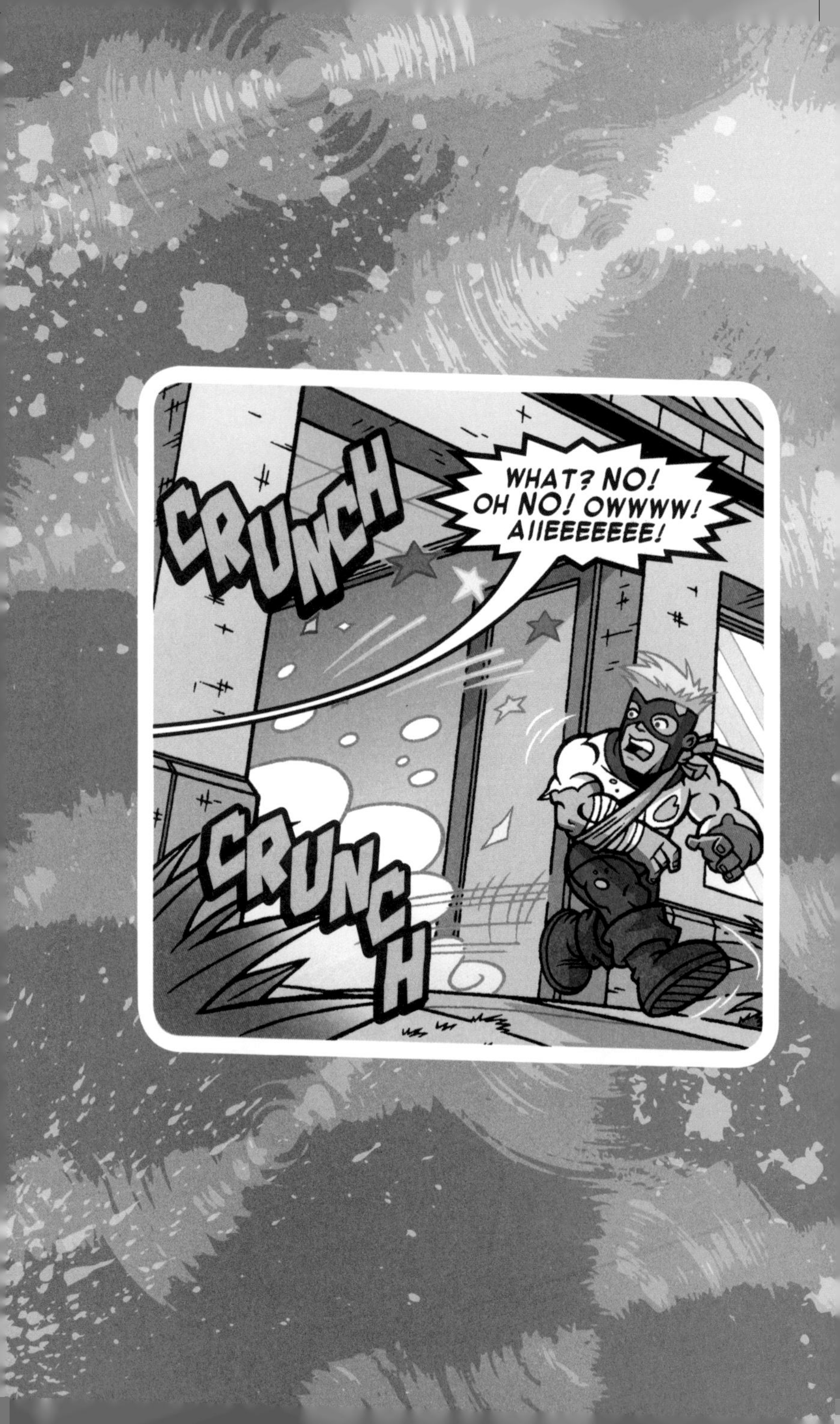
CRUNCH
WHAT? NO! OH NO! OWWWW! AIIEEEEEEE!
CRUNCH

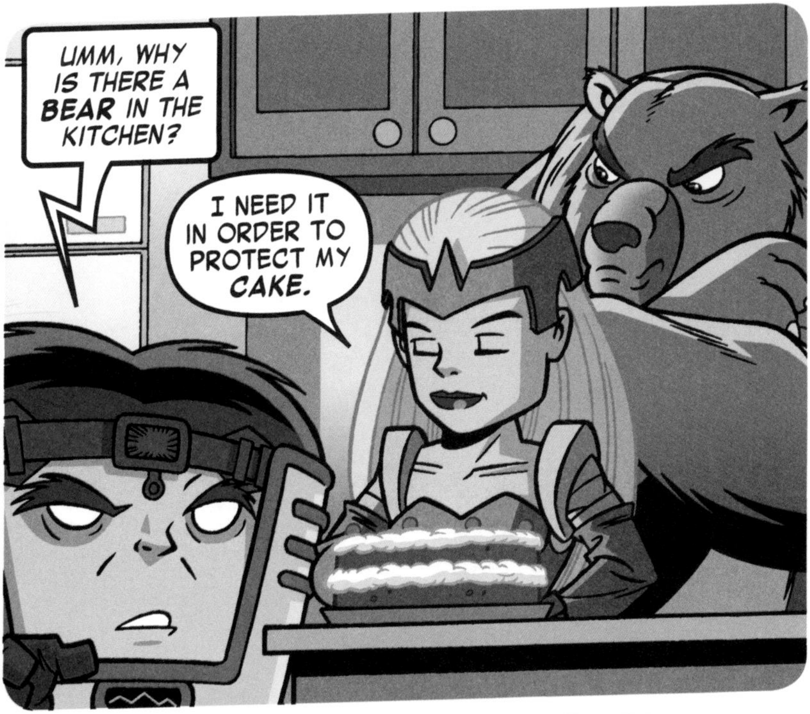
UMM, WHY IS THERE A BEAR IN THE KITCHEN?
I NEED IT IN ORDER TO PROTECT MY CAKE.

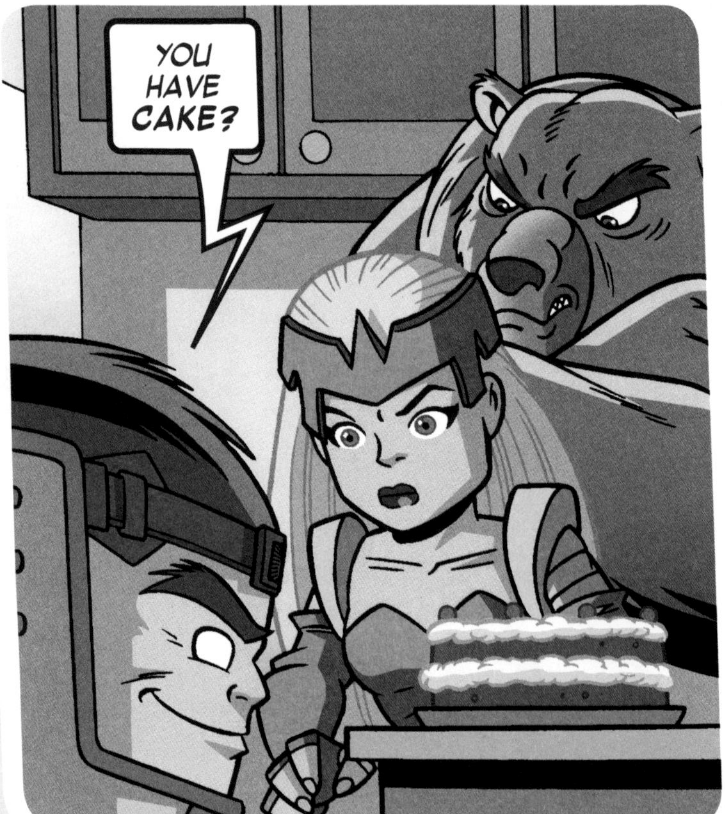
YOU HAVE CAKE?

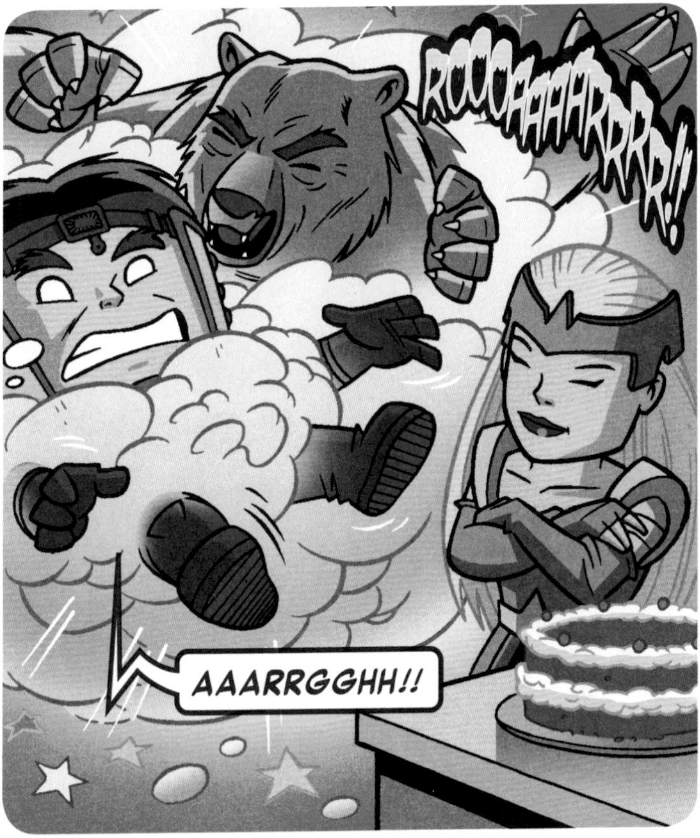
ROOOAAAARRRR!!
AAARRGGHH!!

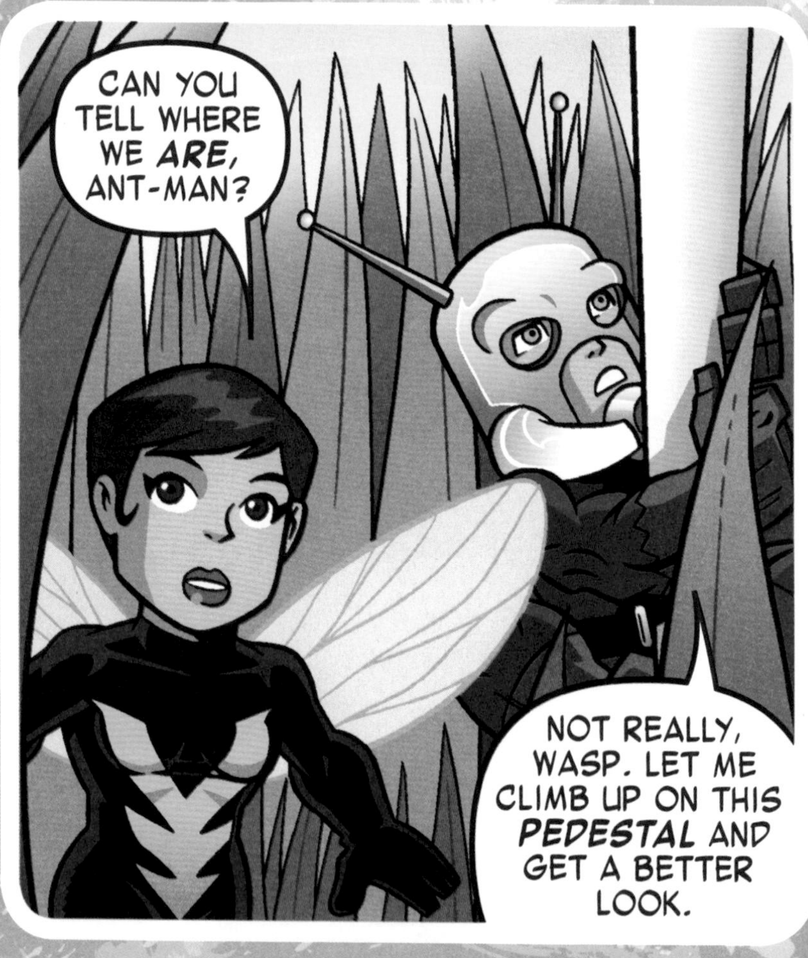
CAN YOU TELL WHERE WE ARE, ANT-MAN?
NOT REALLY, WASP. LET ME CLIMB UP ON THIS PEDESTAL AND GET A BETTER LOOK.

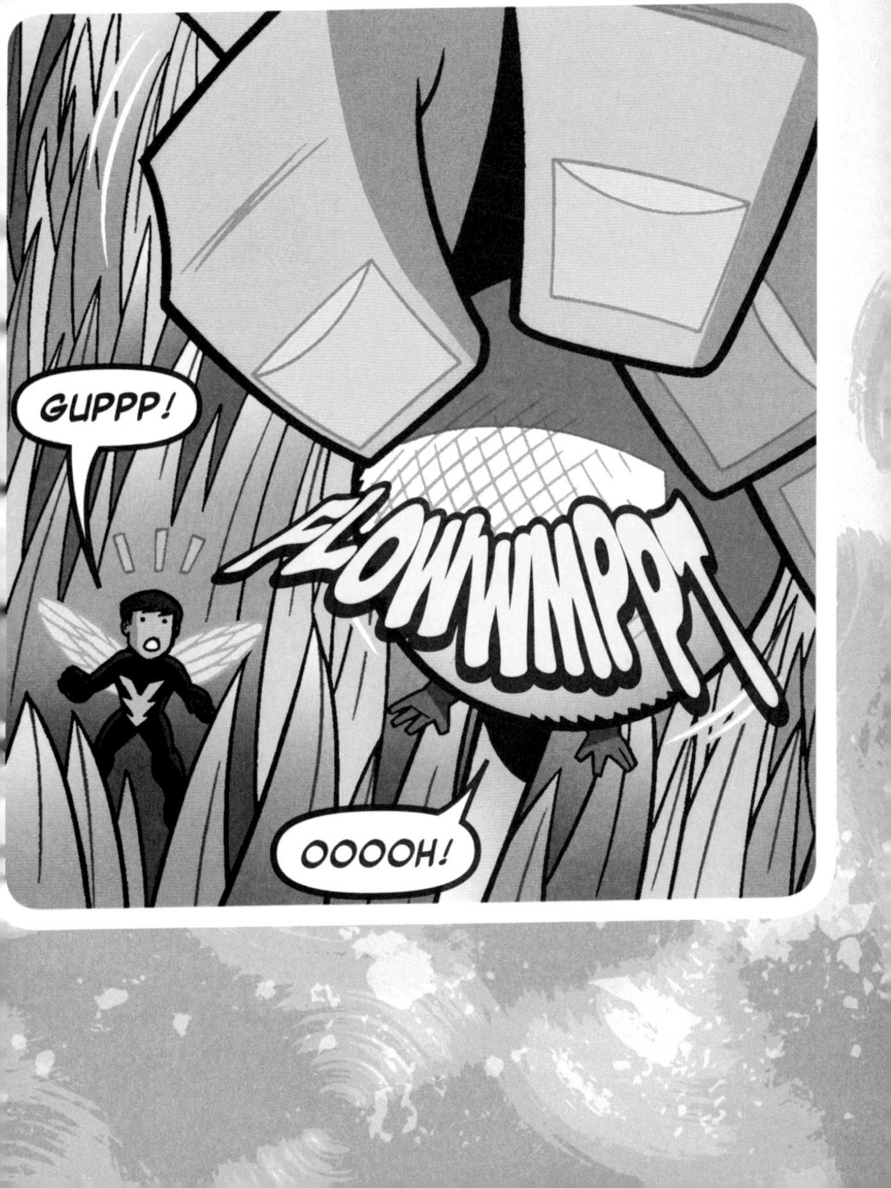
GUPPP!
FLOWWMPPT
OOOOH!

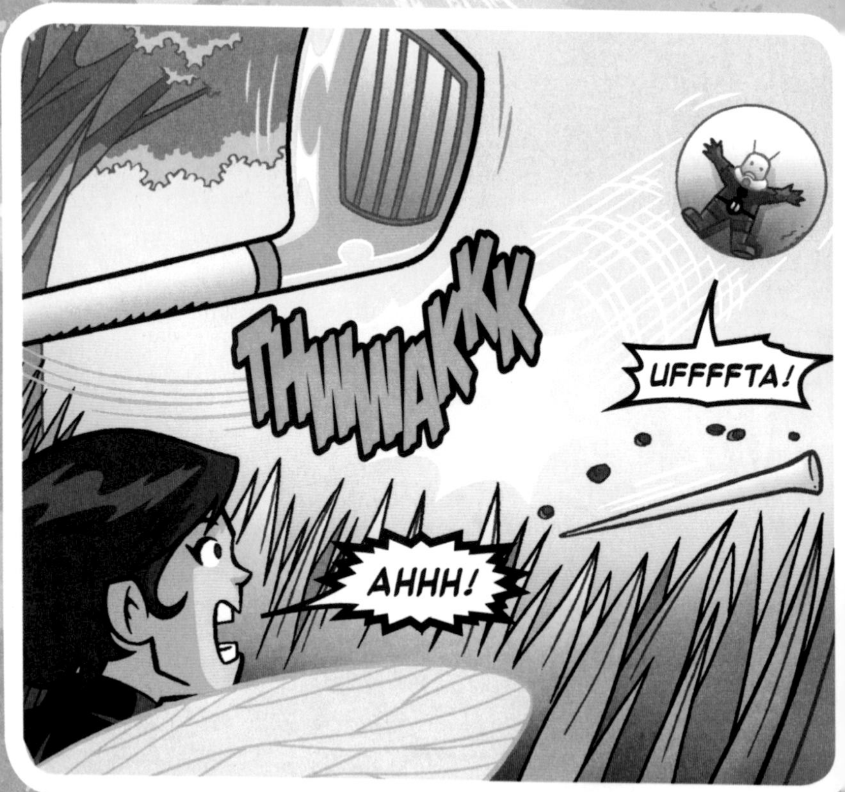
THWWAKKK
UFFFFTA!
AHHH!

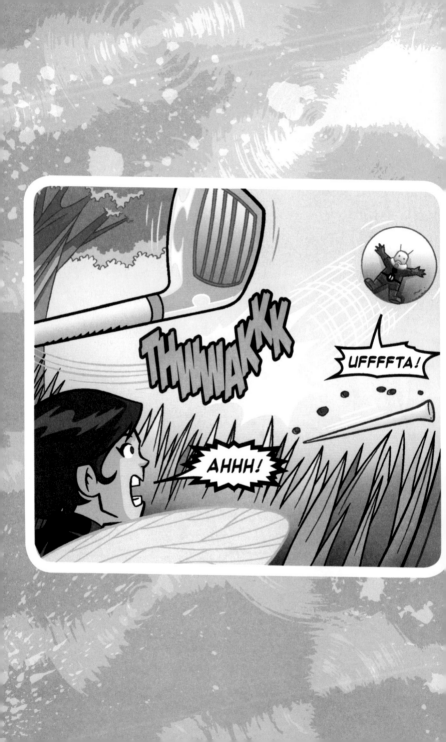

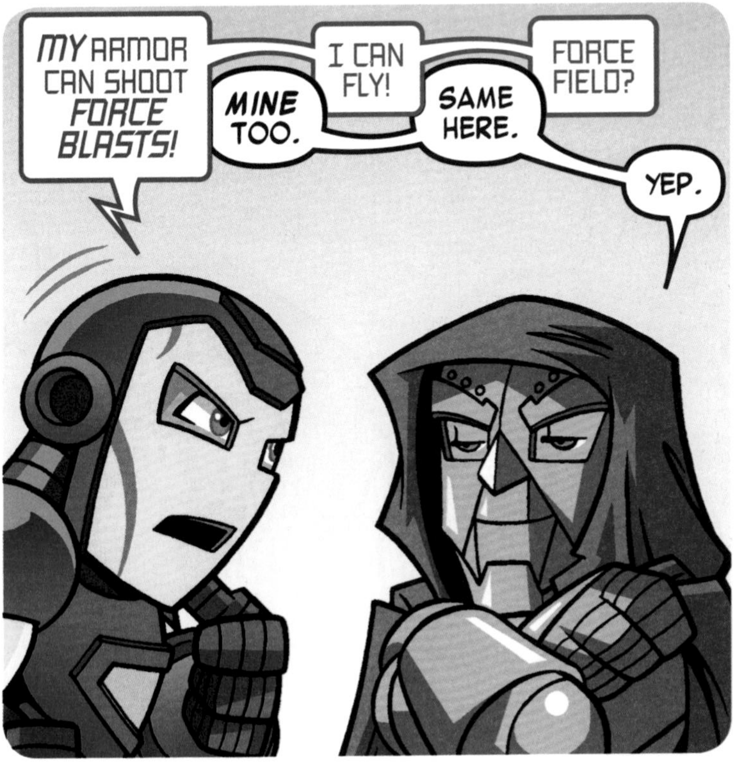
MY ARMOR CAN SHOOT FORCE BLASTS!
MINE TOO.
I CAN FLY!
SAME HERE.
FORCE FIELD?
YEP.

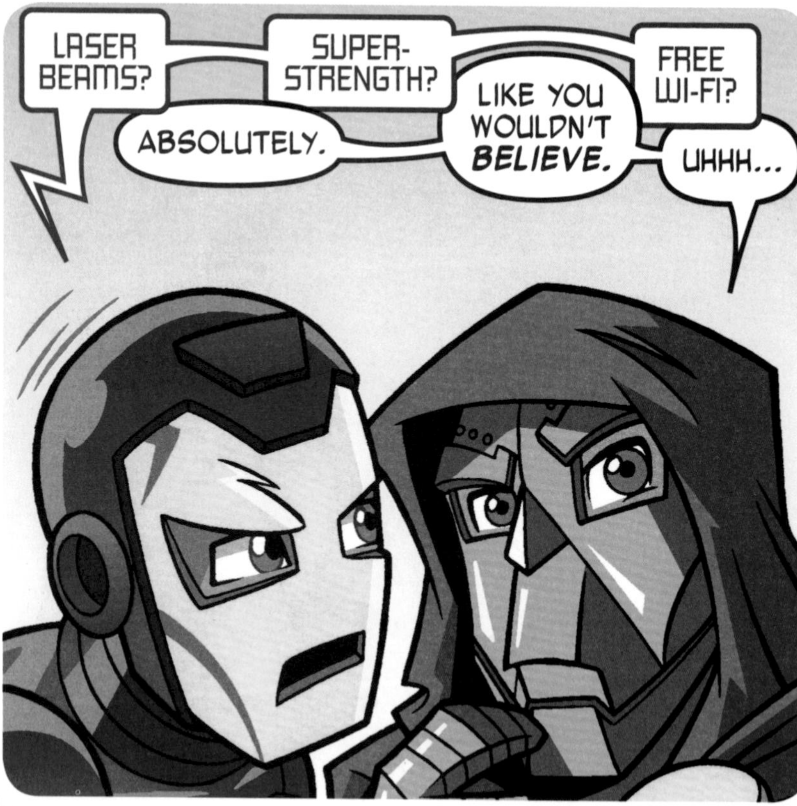
LASER BEAMS?
ABSOLUTELY.
SUPER-STRENGTH?
LIKE YOU WOULDN'T *BELIEVE.*
FREE WI-FI?
UHHH...

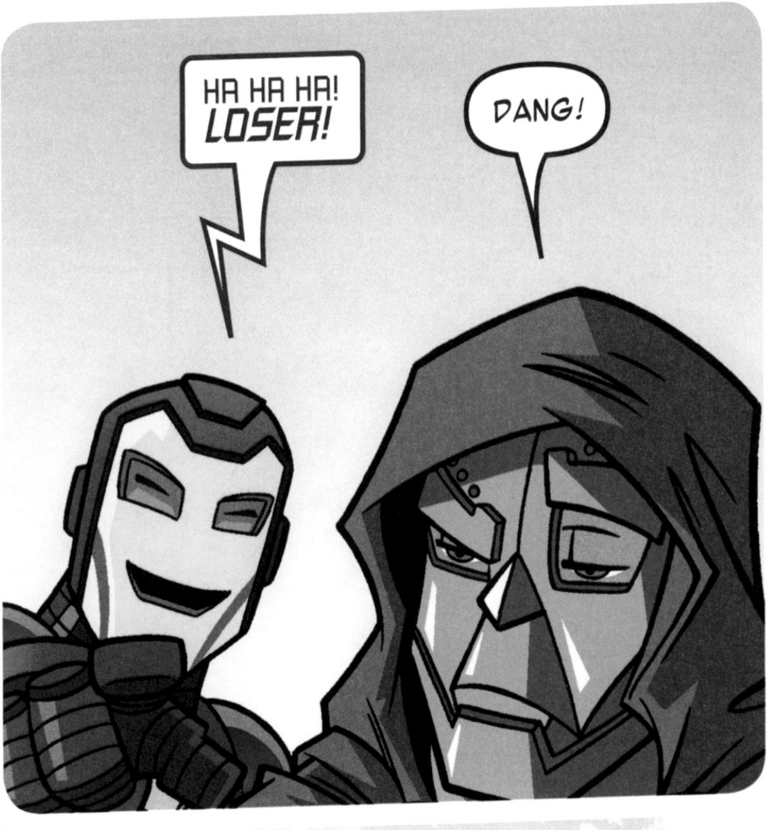
HA HA HA!
LOSER!
DANG!

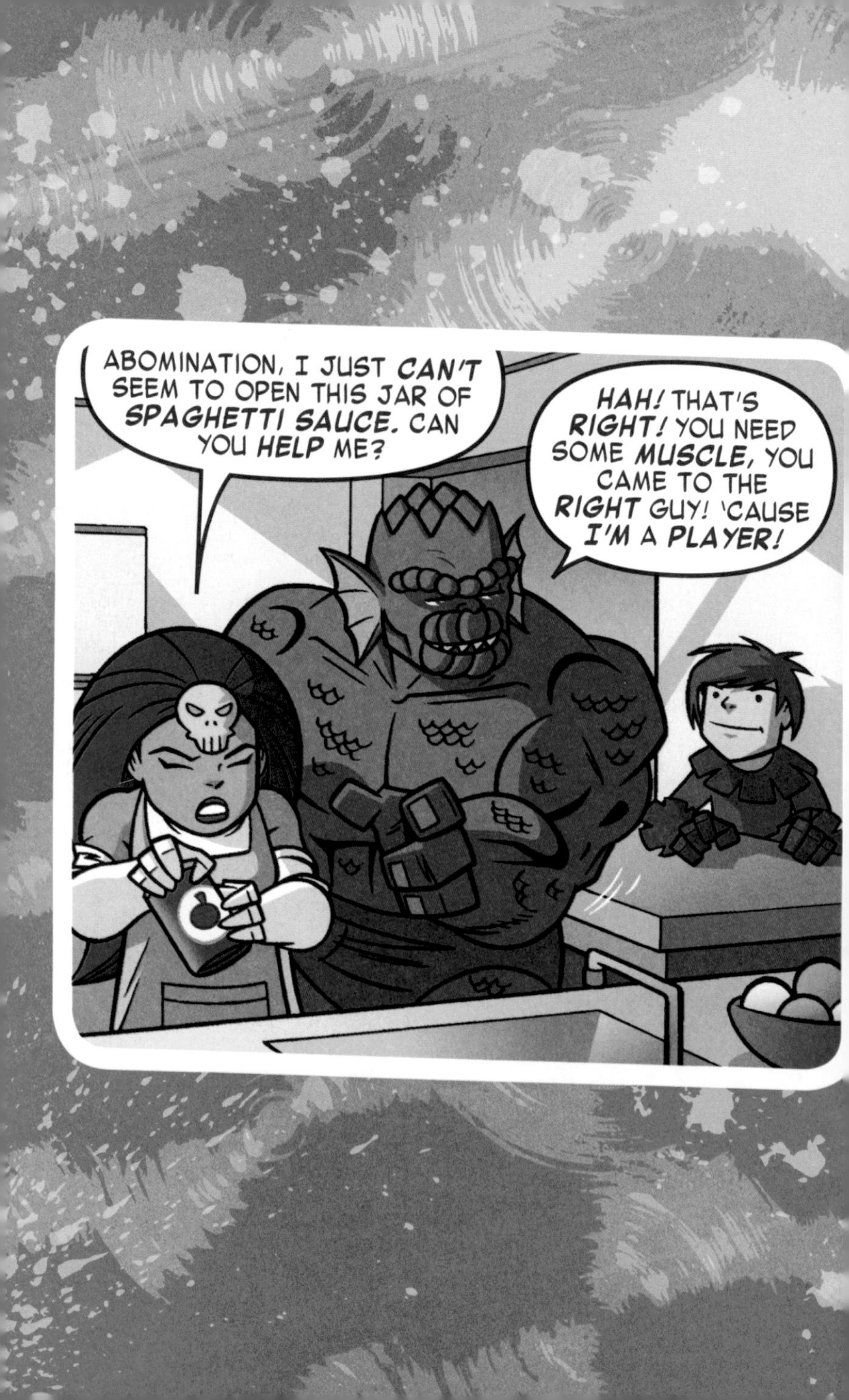
ABOMINATION, I JUST CAN'T SEEM TO OPEN THIS JAR OF SPAGHETTI SAUCE. CAN YOU HELP ME?
HAH! THAT'S RIGHT! YOU NEED SOME MUSCLE, YOU CAME TO THE RIGHT GUY! 'CAUSE I'M A PLAYER!

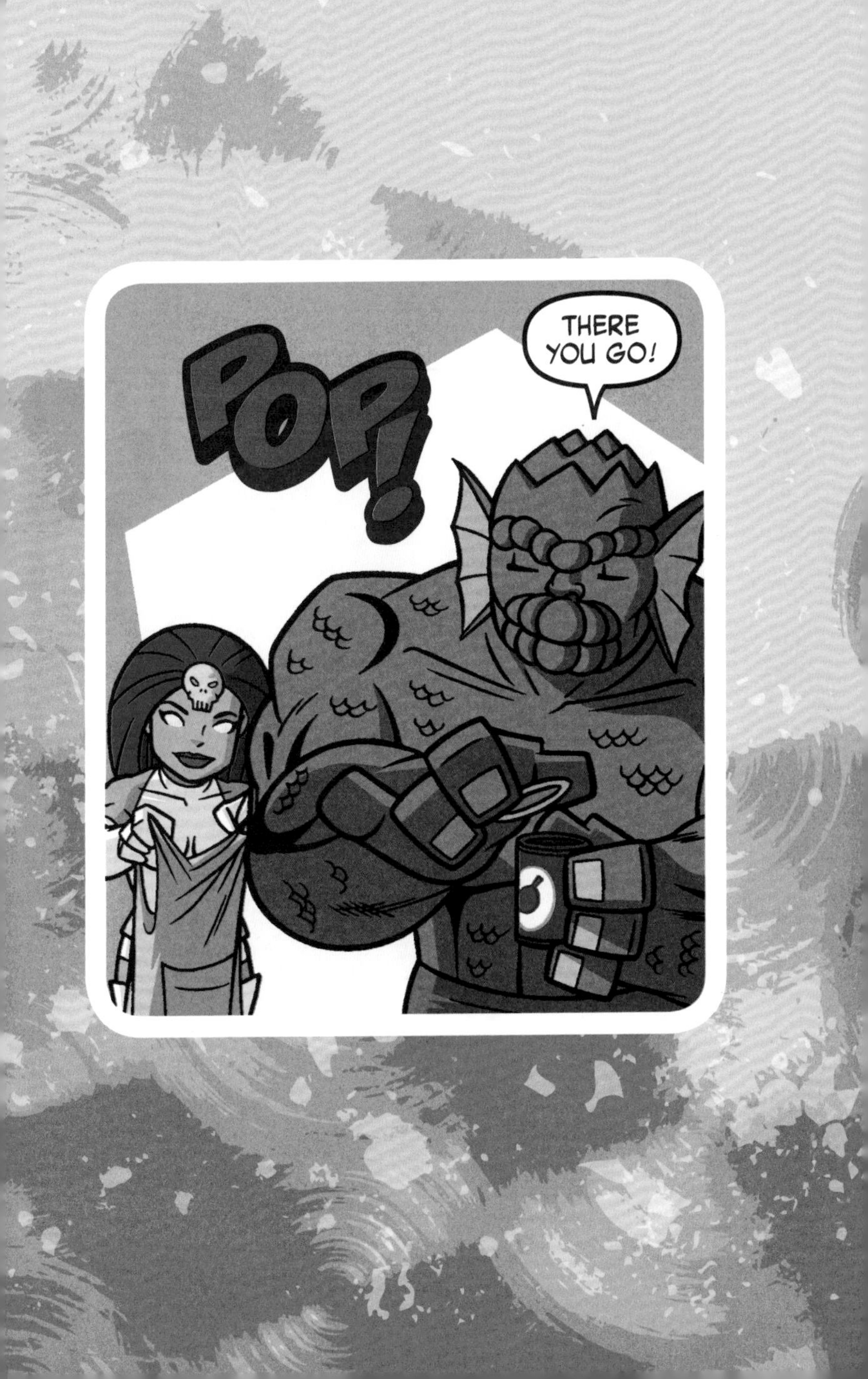
POP!
THERE YOU GO!

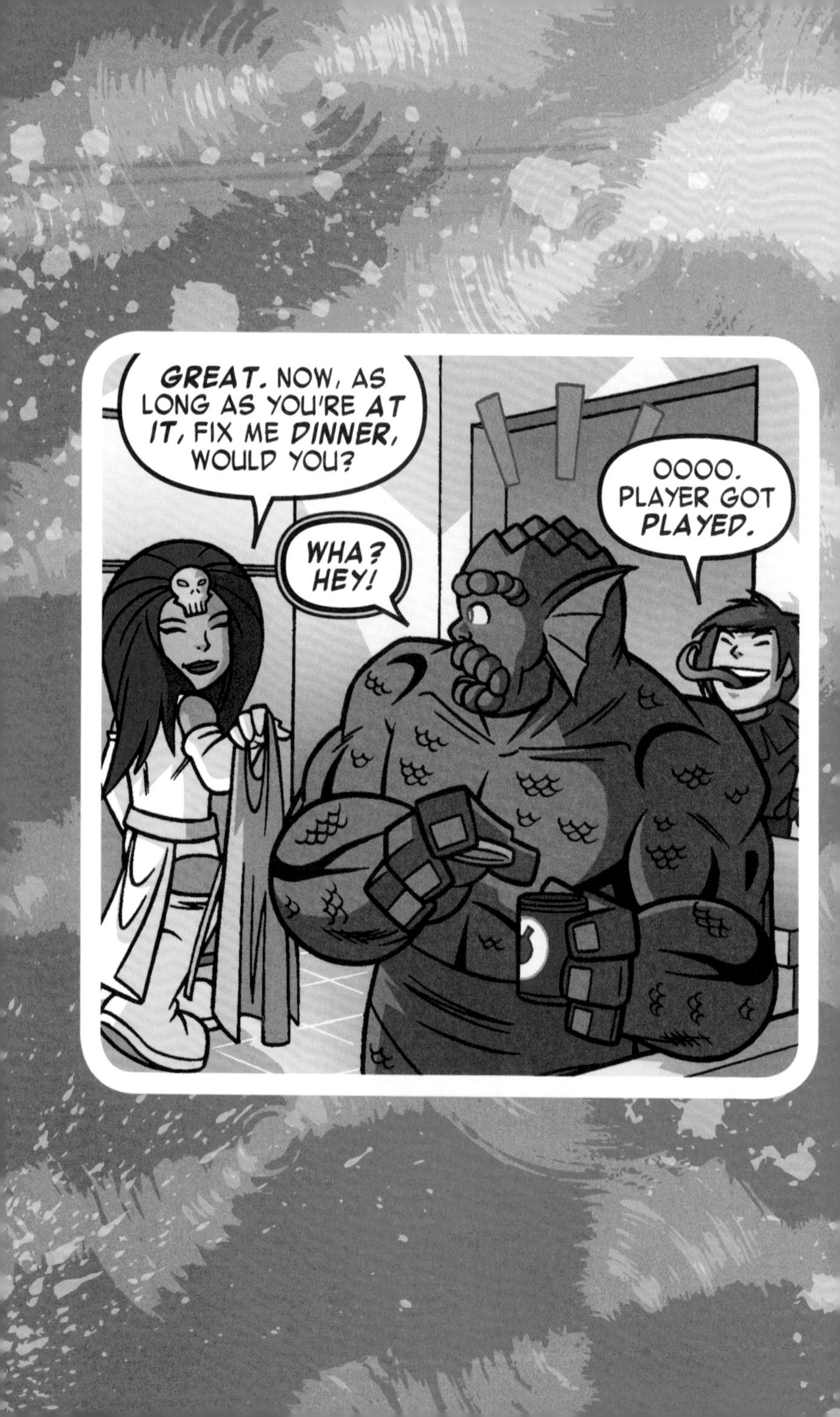
GREAT. NOW, AS LONG AS YOU'RE AT IT, FIX ME DINNER, WOULD YOU?
WHA? HEY!
OOOO. PLAYER GOT PLAYED.

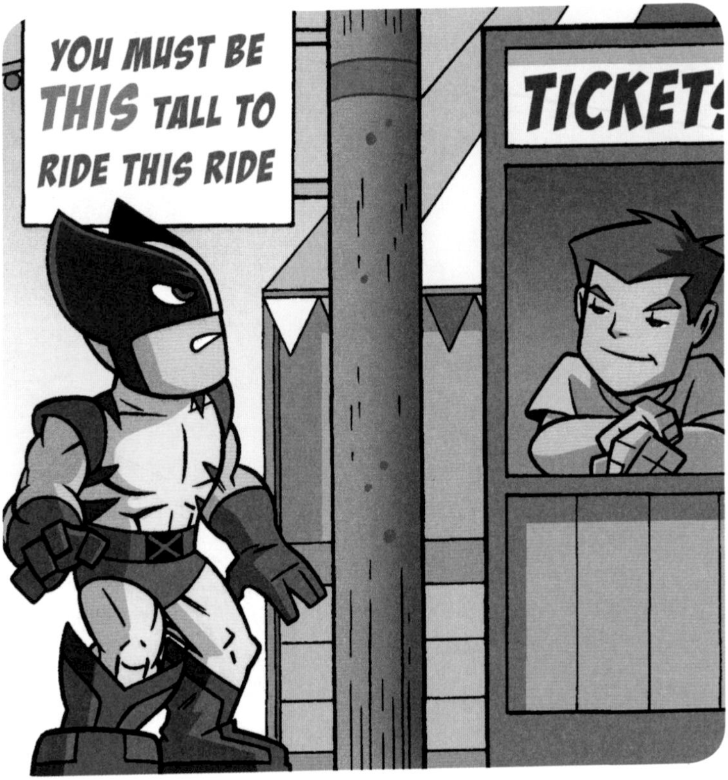
YOU MUST BE THIS TALL TO RIDE THIS RIDE
TICKETS

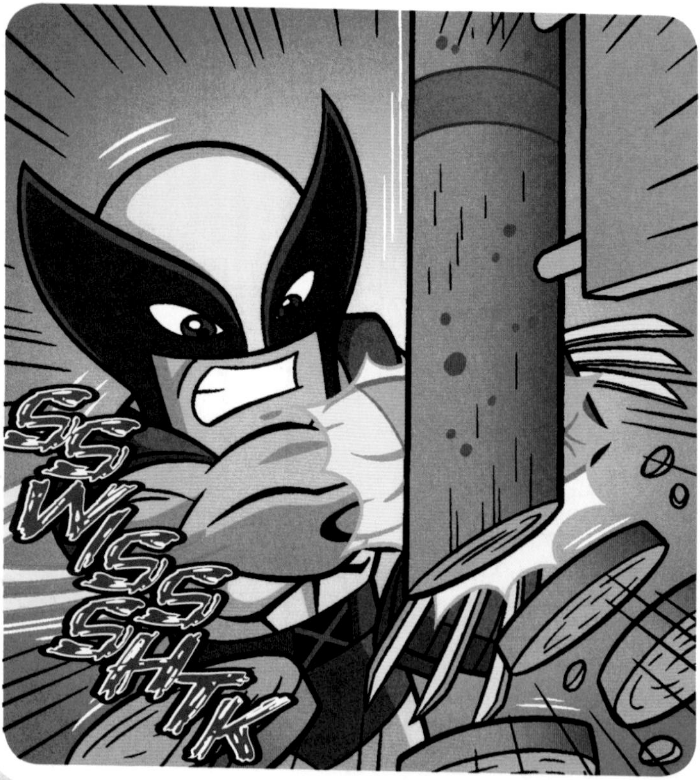
SSWISSSHTK

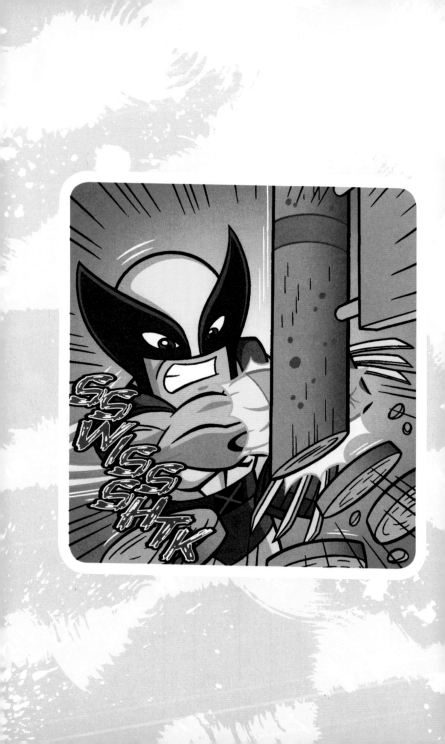

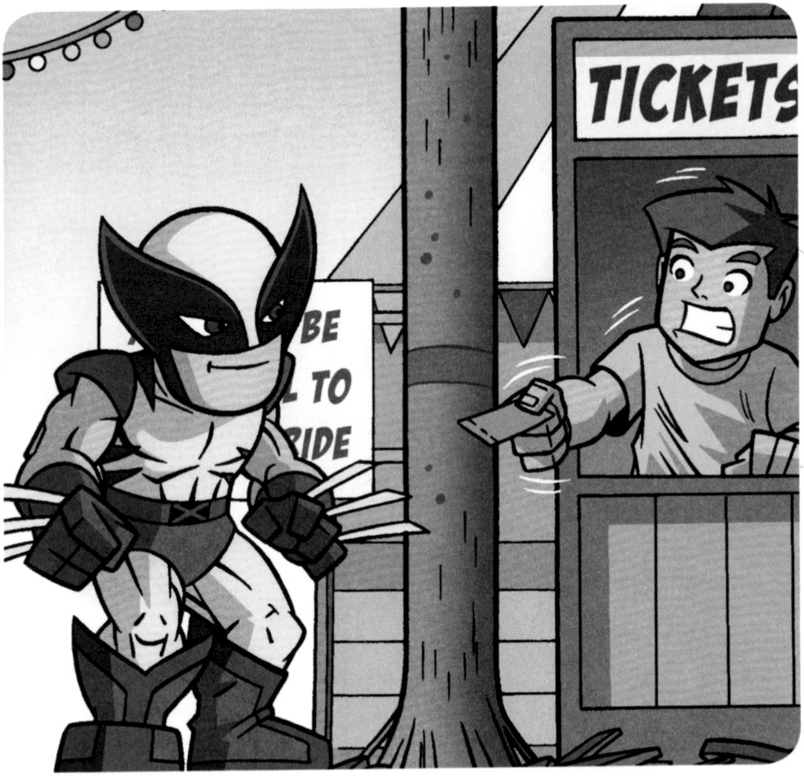
TICKETS

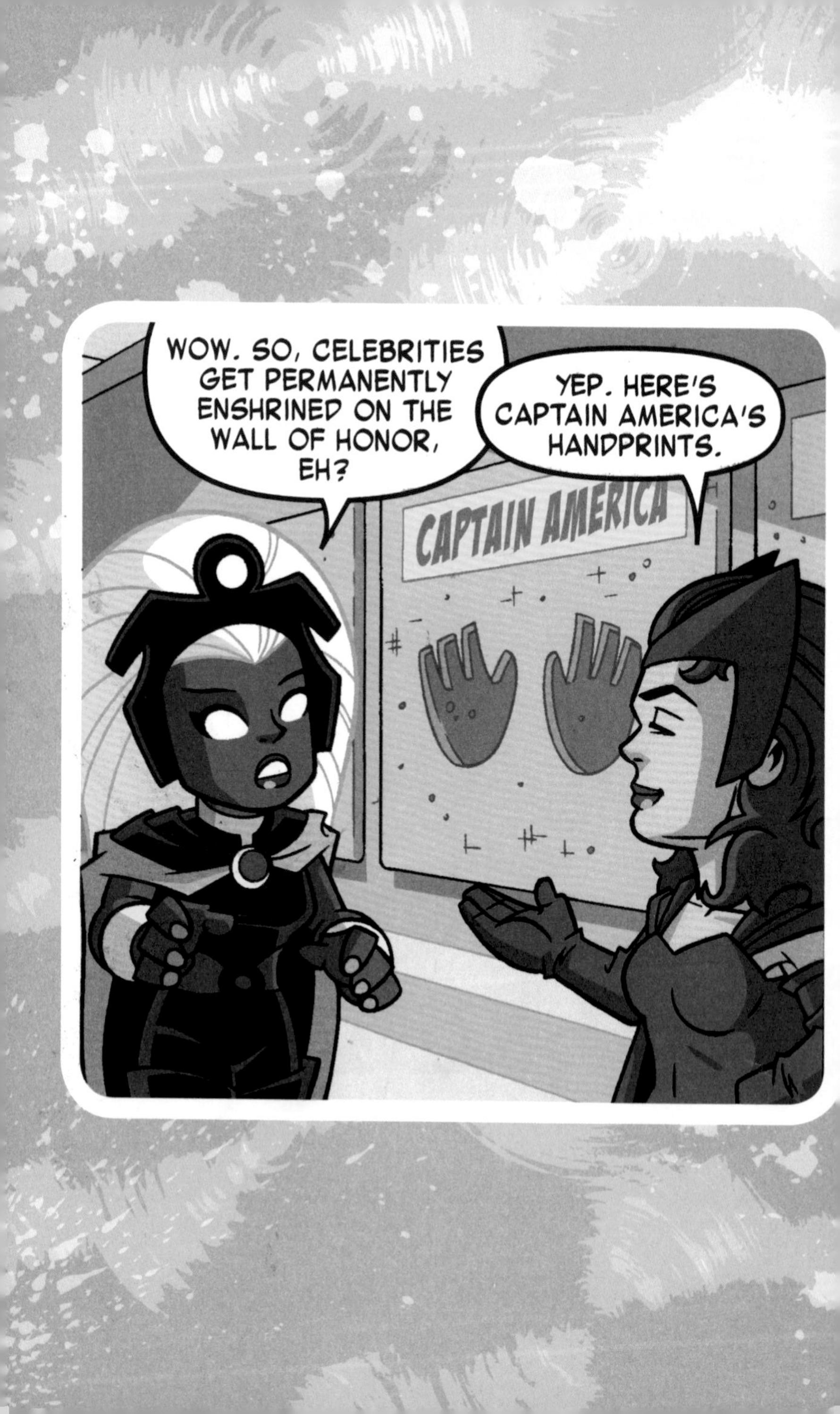
WOW. SO, CELEBRITIES GET PERMANENTLY ENSHRINED ON THE WALL OF HONOR, EH?
YEP. HERE'S CAPTAIN AMERICA'S HANDPRINTS.
CAPTAIN AMERICA

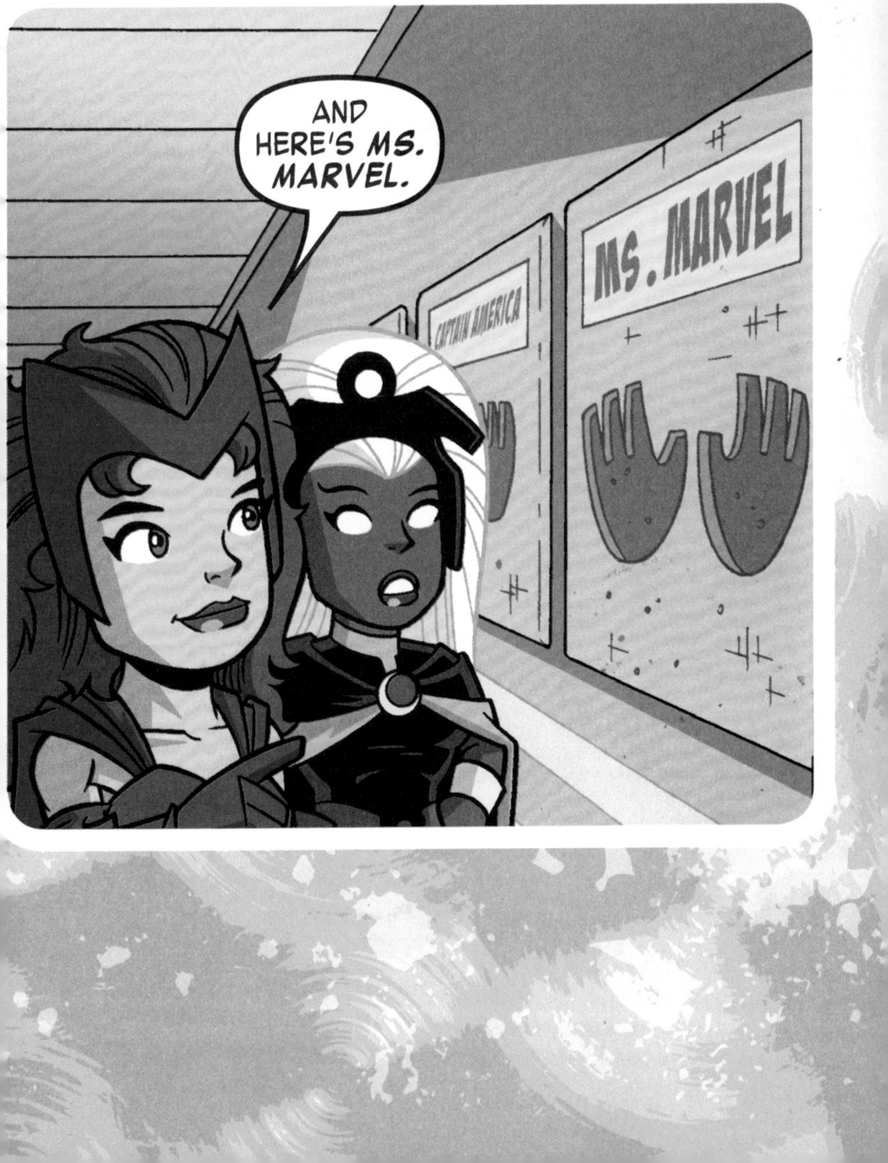
AND HERE'S *MS. MARVEL.*
MS. MARVEL
CAPTAIN AMERICA

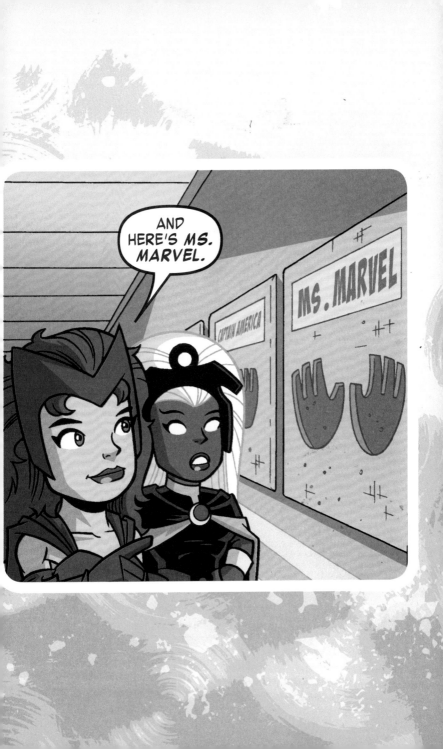

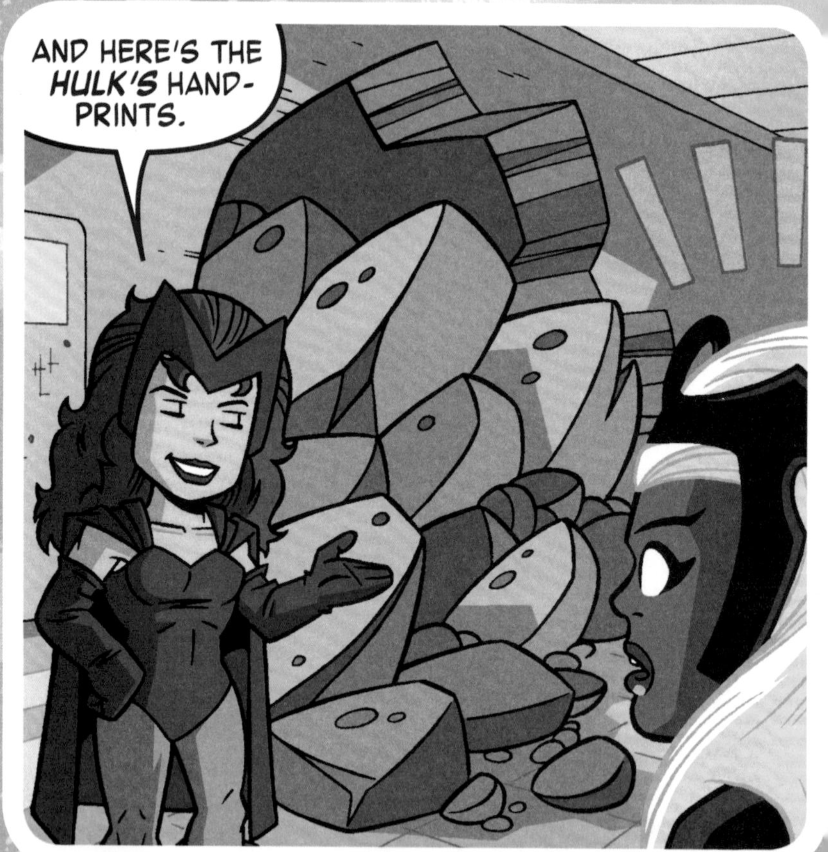
AND HERE'S THE *HULK'S* HAND-PRINTS.

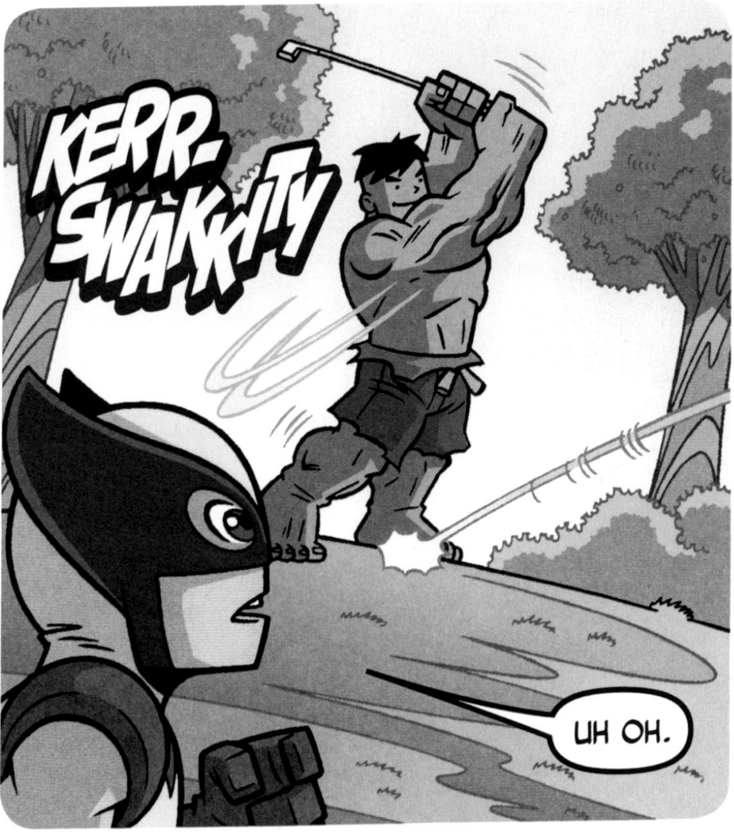
KERR-SWAKK-ITY
UH OH.

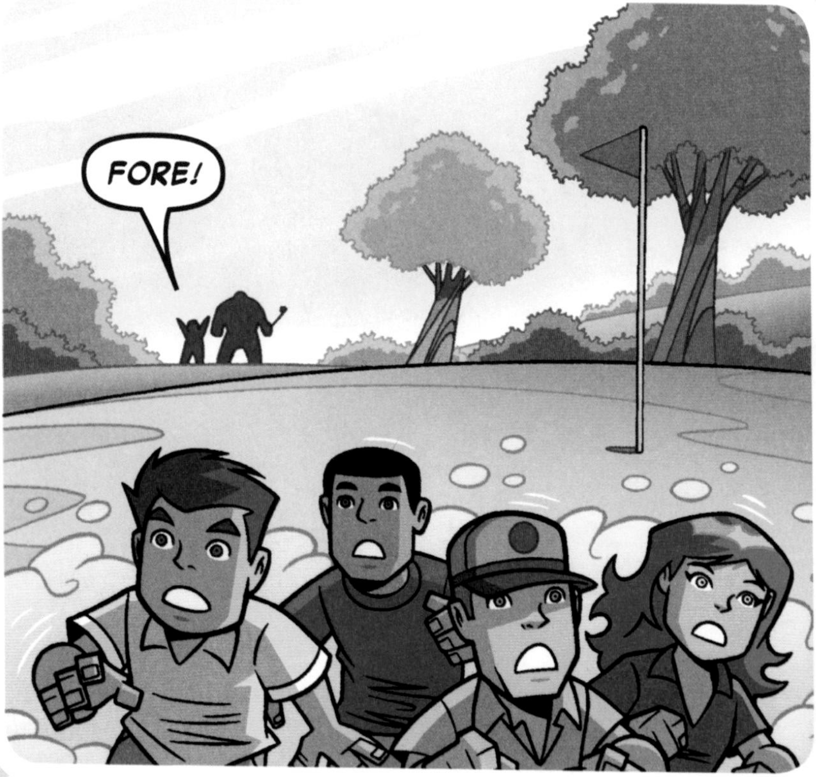
FORE!

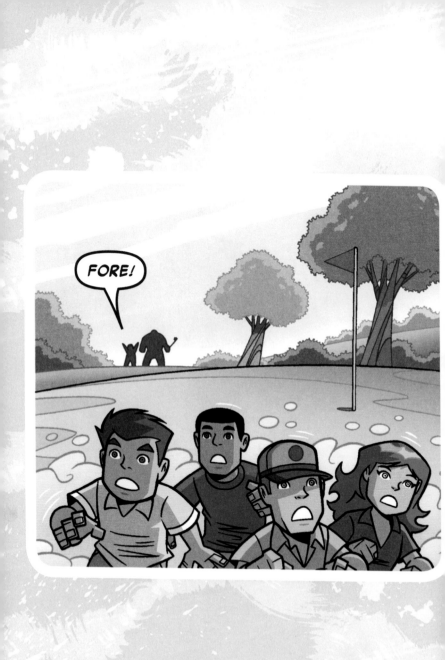

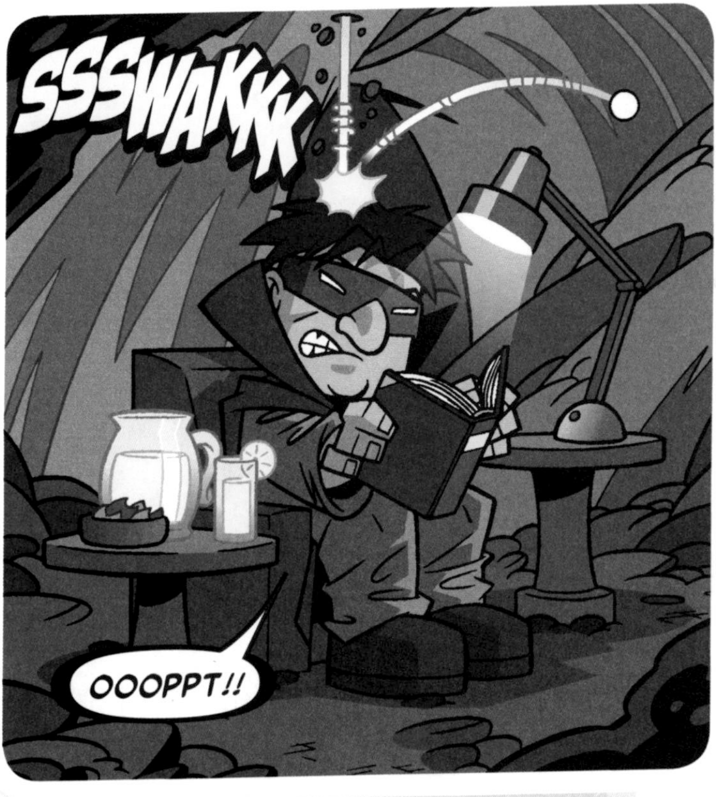
SSSWAKKK
OOOPPT!!

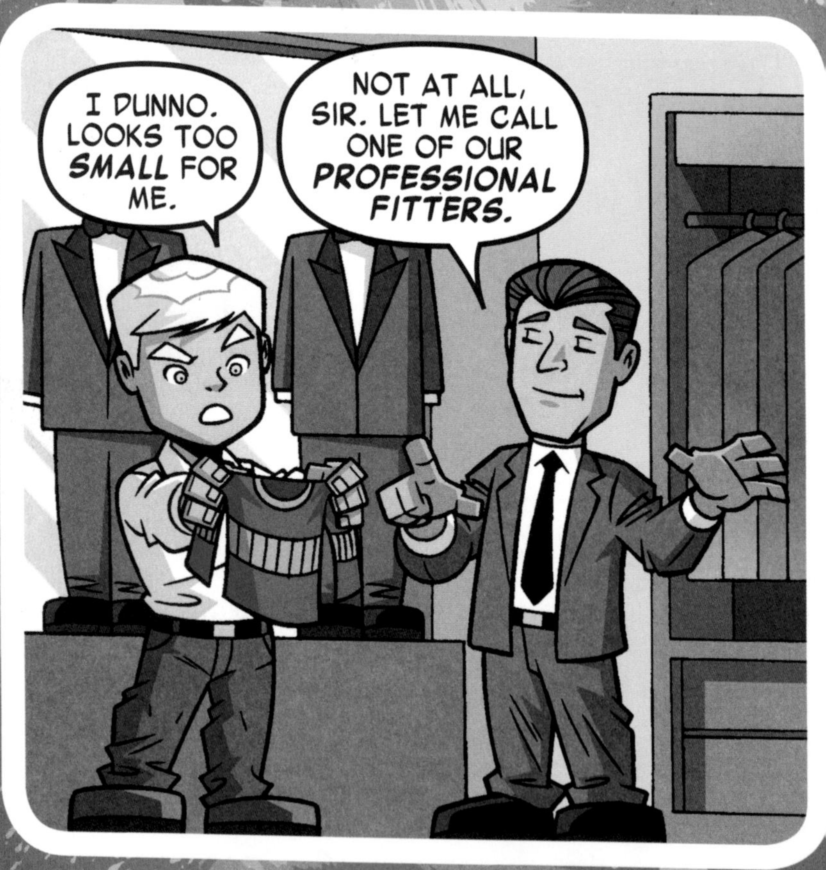
I DUNNO. LOOKS TOO SMALL FOR ME.
NOT AT ALL, SIR. LET ME CALL ONE OF OUR PROFESSIONAL FITTERS.

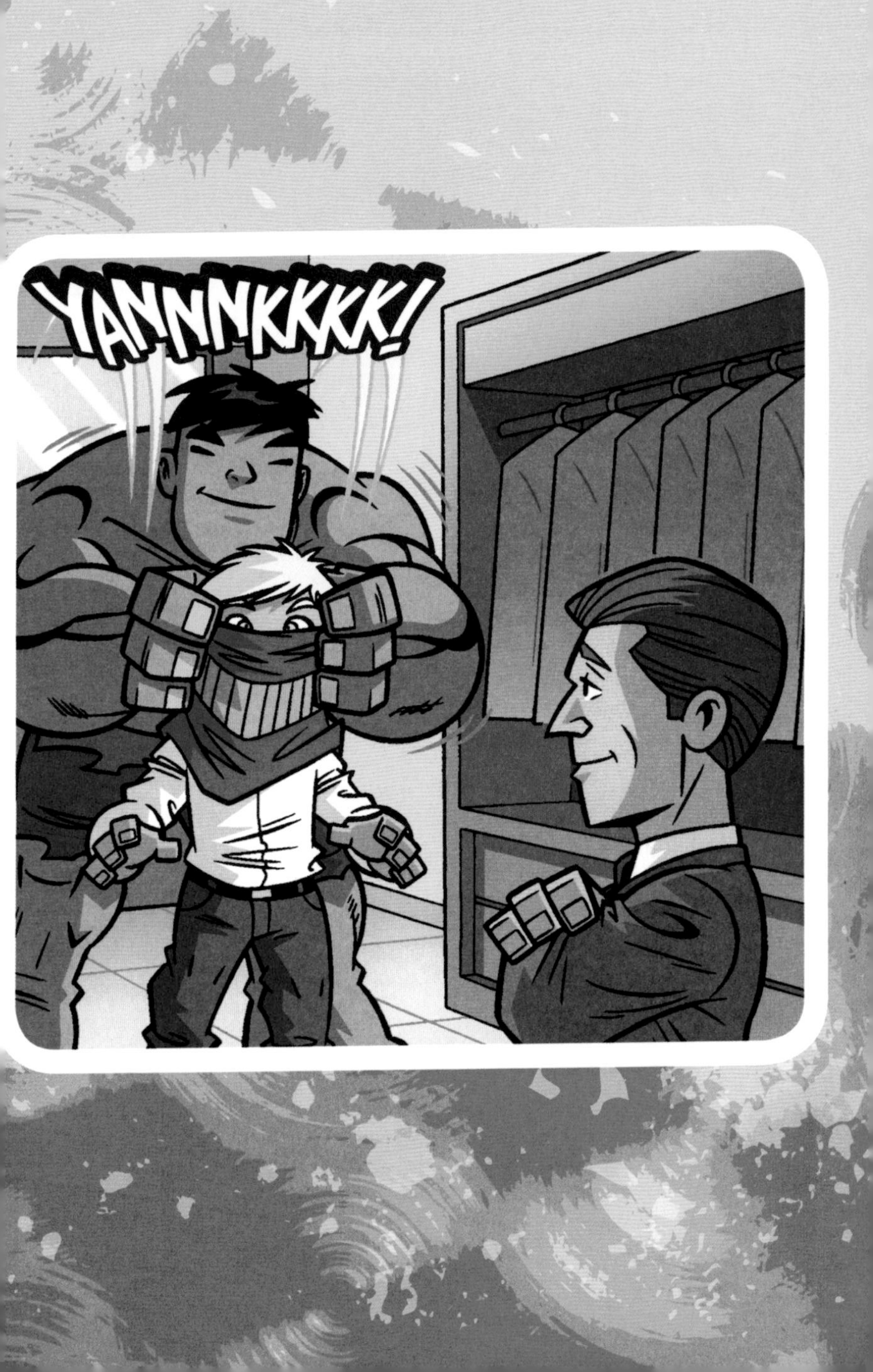
YANNNKKKK!

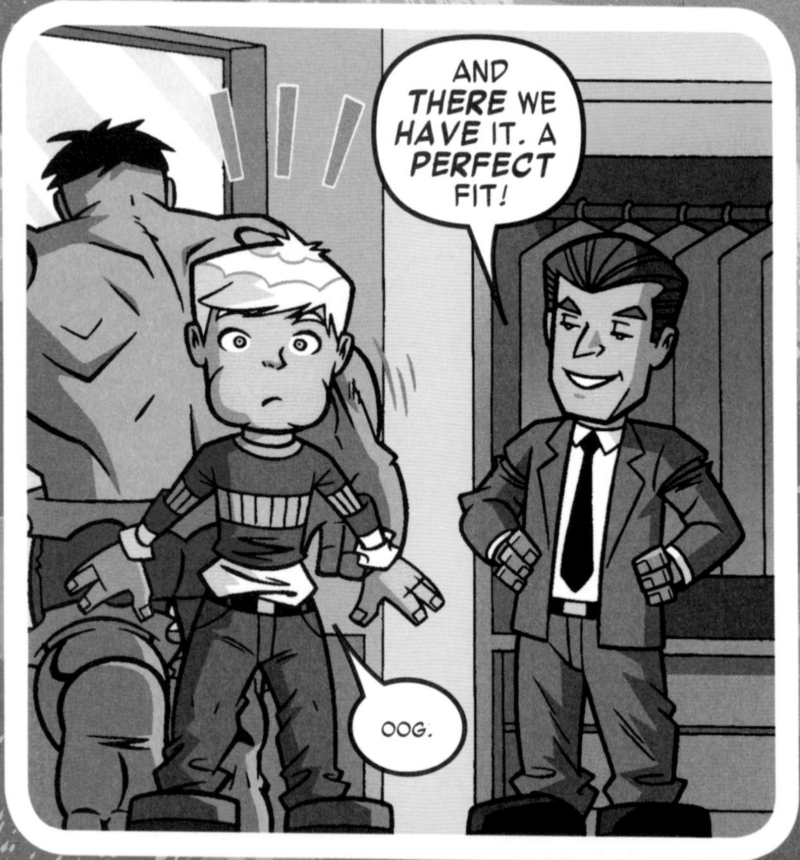
AND THERE WE HAVE IT. A PERFECT FIT!
OOG.

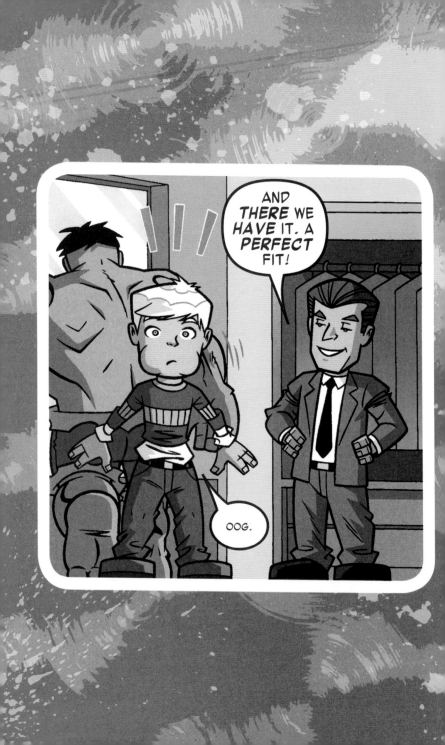

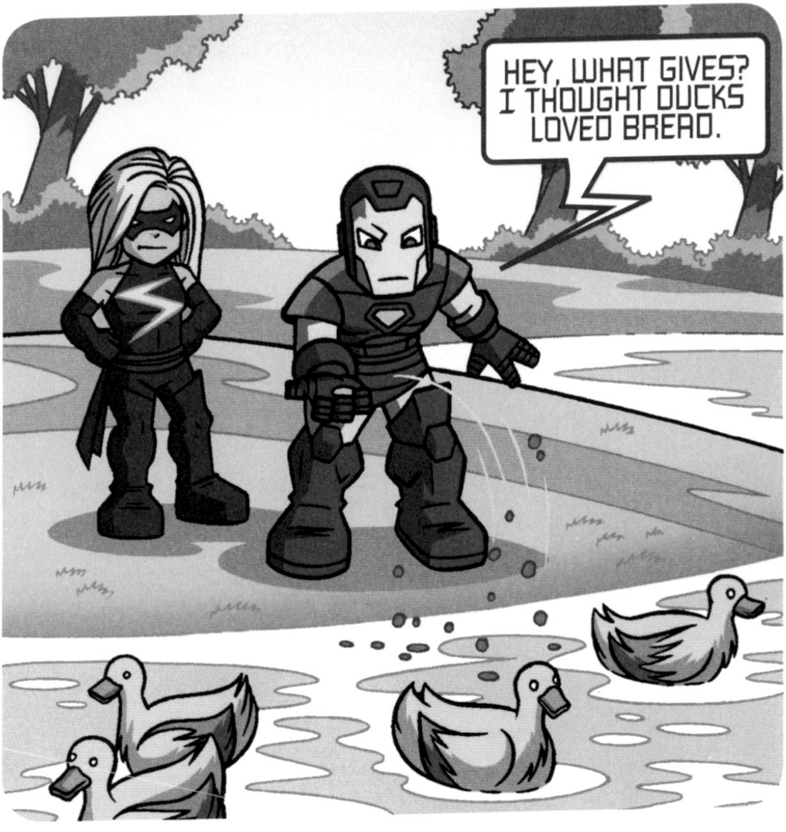
HEY, WHAT GIVES? I THOUGHT DUCKS LOVED BREAD.

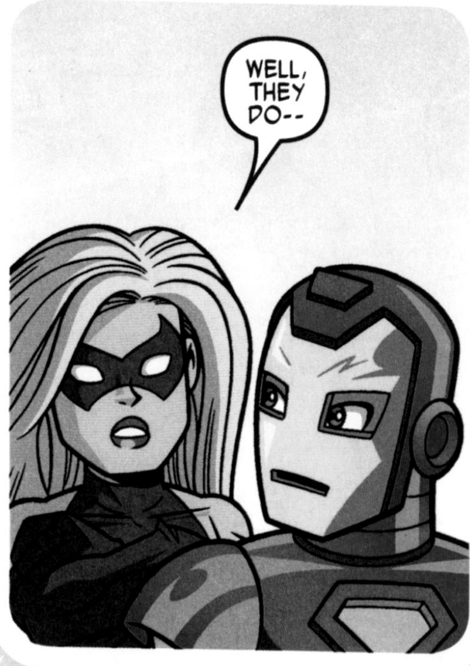
WELL, THEY DO--

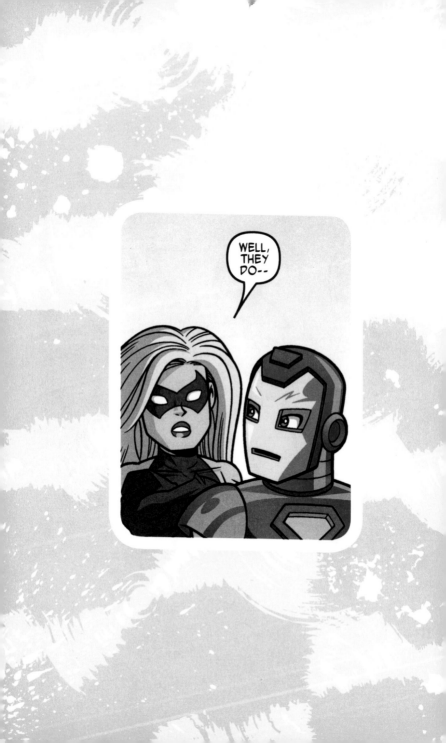

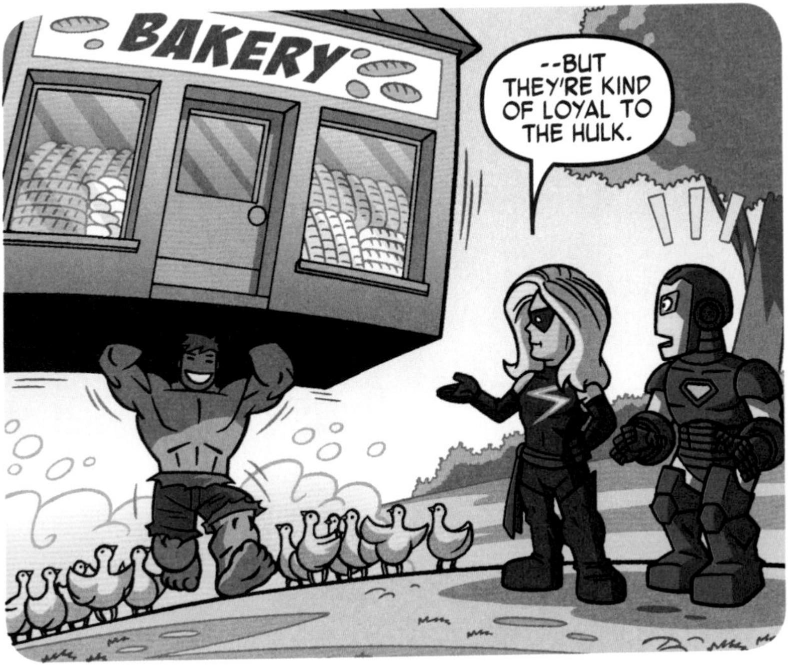
BAKERY
--BUT THEY'RE KIND OF LOYAL TO THE HULK.

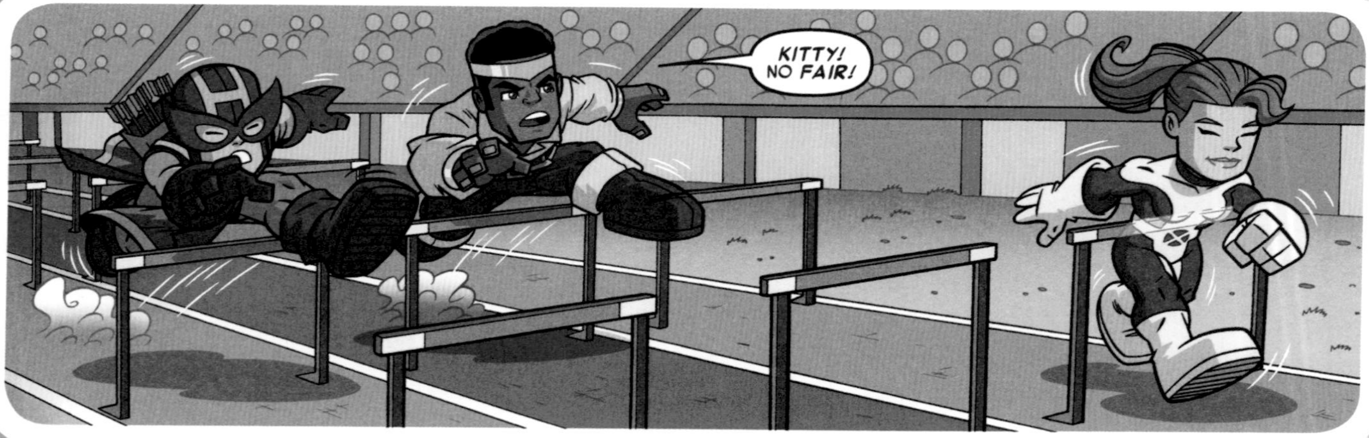
KITTY! NO FAIR!

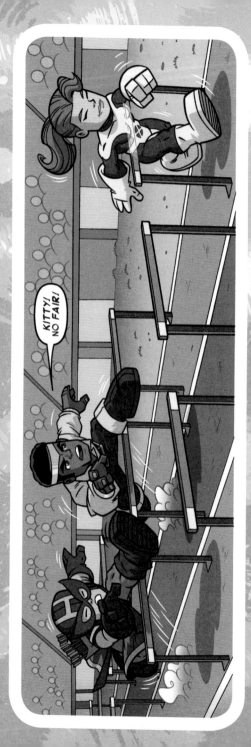

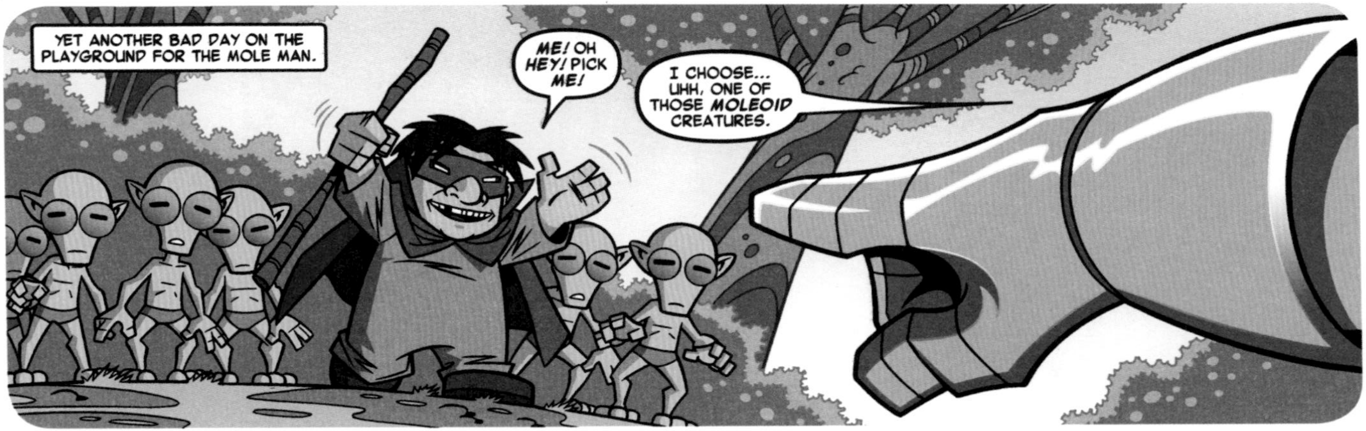
YET ANOTHER BAD DAY ON THE PLAYGROUND FOR THE MOLE MAN.
ME! OH *HEY!* PICK *ME!*
I CHOOSE... UHH, ONE OF THOSE *MOLEOID* CREATURES.

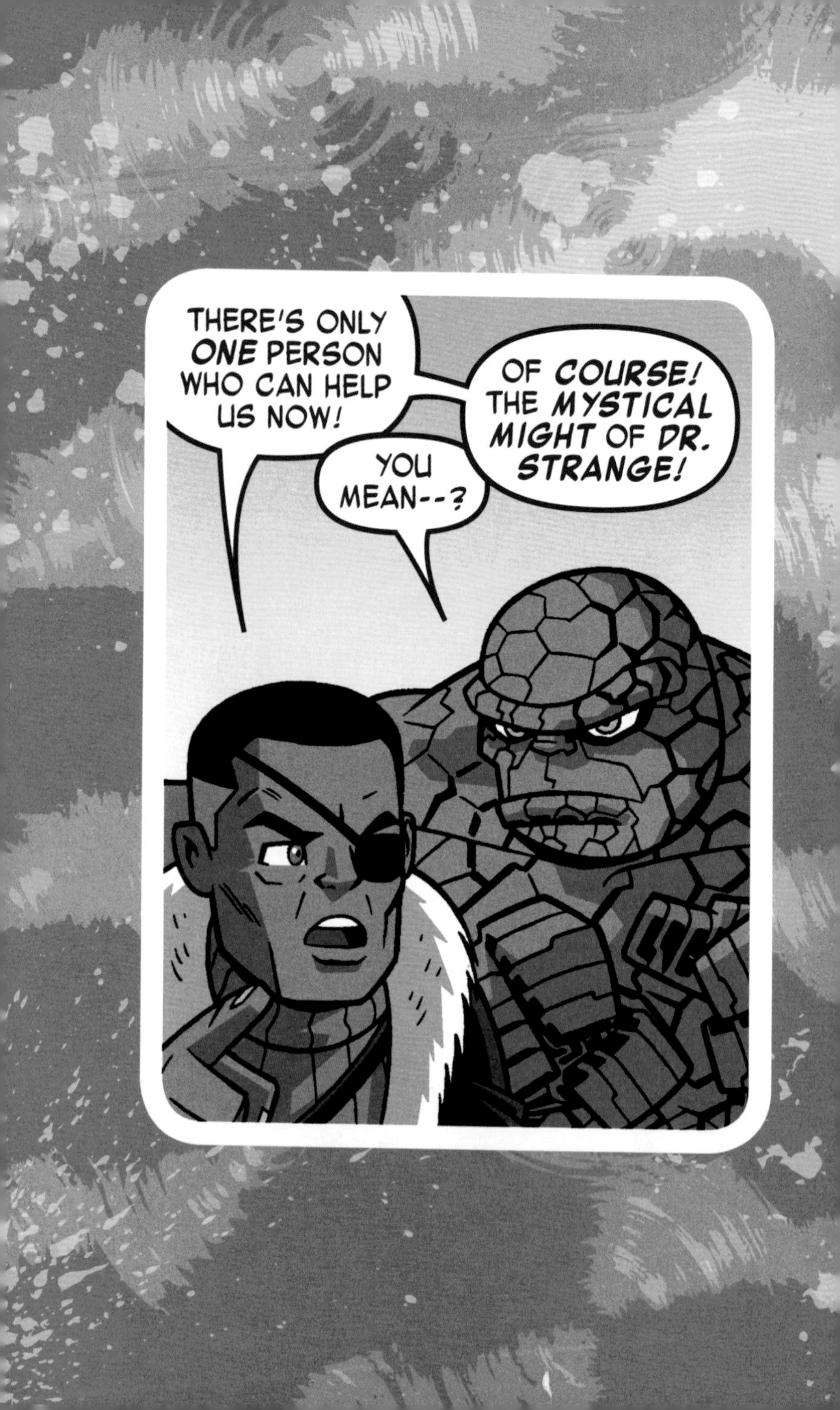
THERE'S ONLY ONE PERSON WHO CAN HELP US NOW!
YOU MEAN--?
OF COURSE! THE MYSTICAL MIGHT OF DR. STRANGE!

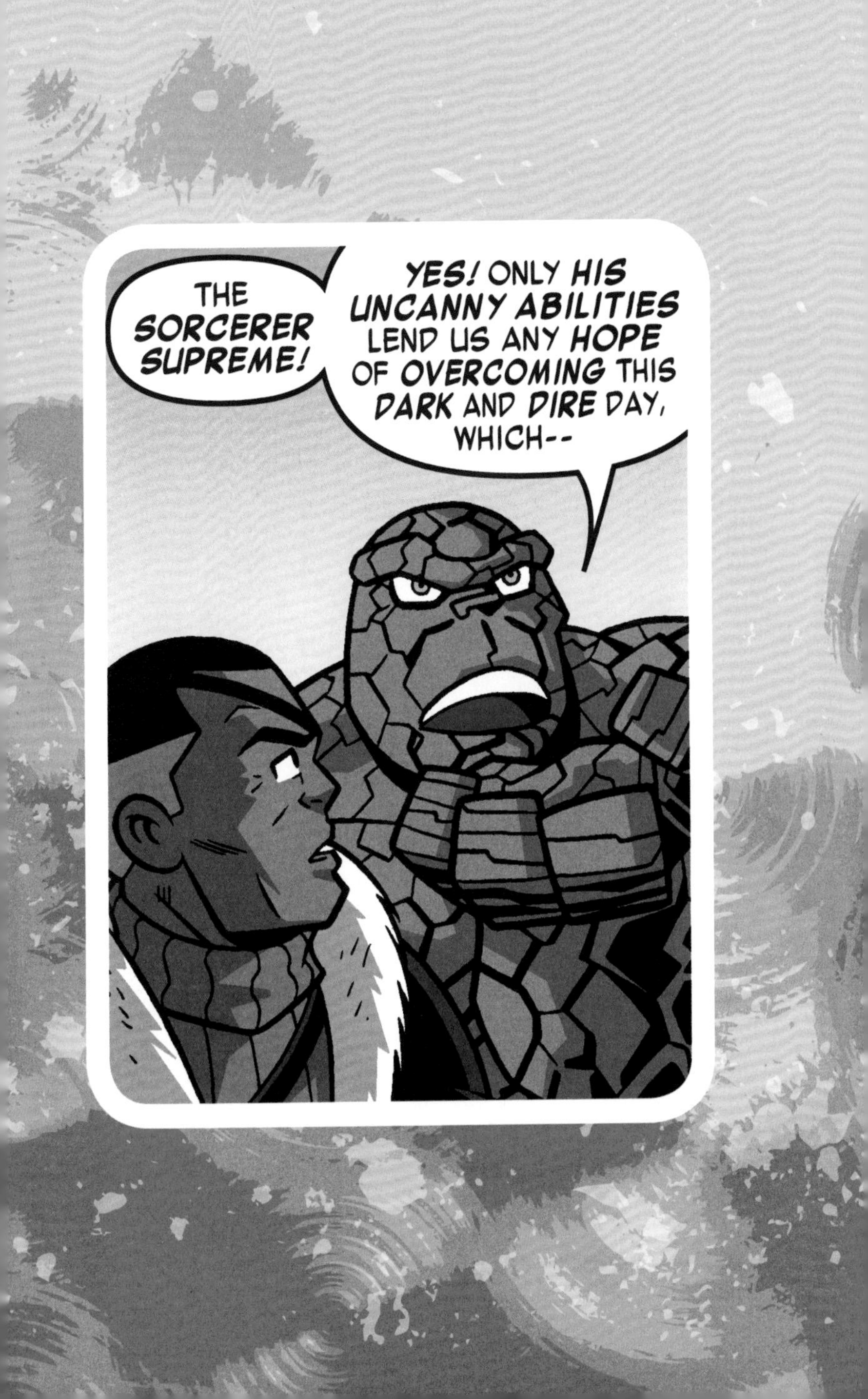
THE SORCERER SUPREME!
YES! ONLY HIS UNCANNY ABILITIES LEND US ANY HOPE OF OVERCOMING THIS DARK AND DIRE DAY, WHICH--

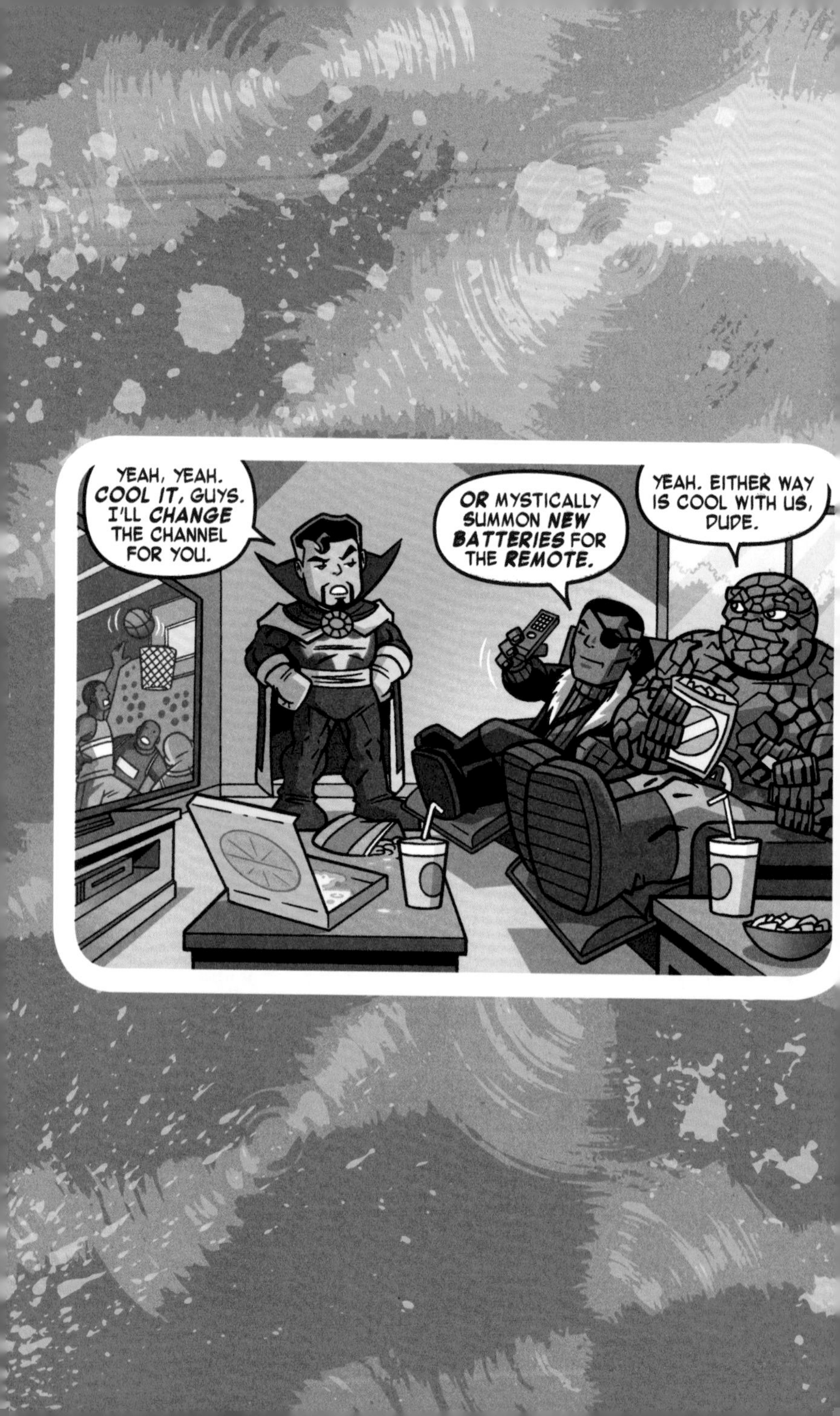
YEAH, YEAH. COOL IT, GUYS. I'LL CHANGE THE CHANNEL FOR YOU.
OR MYSTICALLY SUMMON NEW BATTERIES FOR THE REMOTE.
YEAH. EITHER WAY IS COOL WITH US, DUDE.

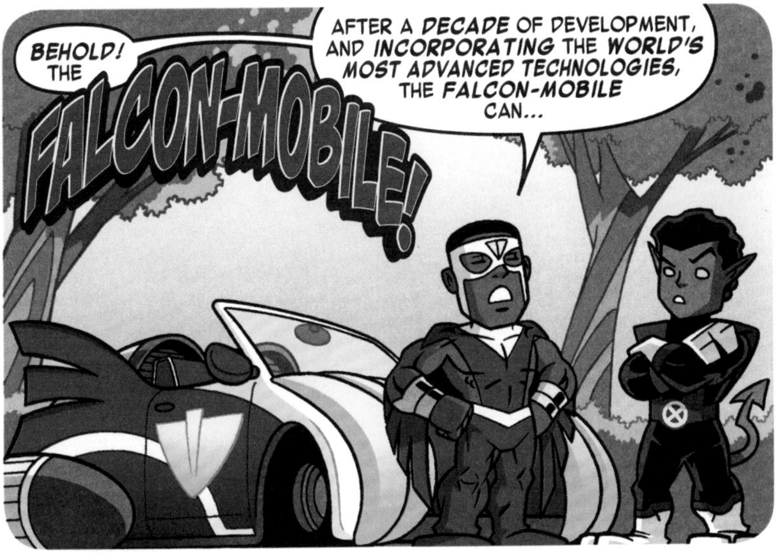
BEHOLD! THE
FALCON-MOBILE!
AFTER A DECADE OF DEVELOPMENT, AND INCORPORATING THE WORLD'S MOST ADVANCED TECHNOLOGIES, THE FALCON-MOBILE CAN...

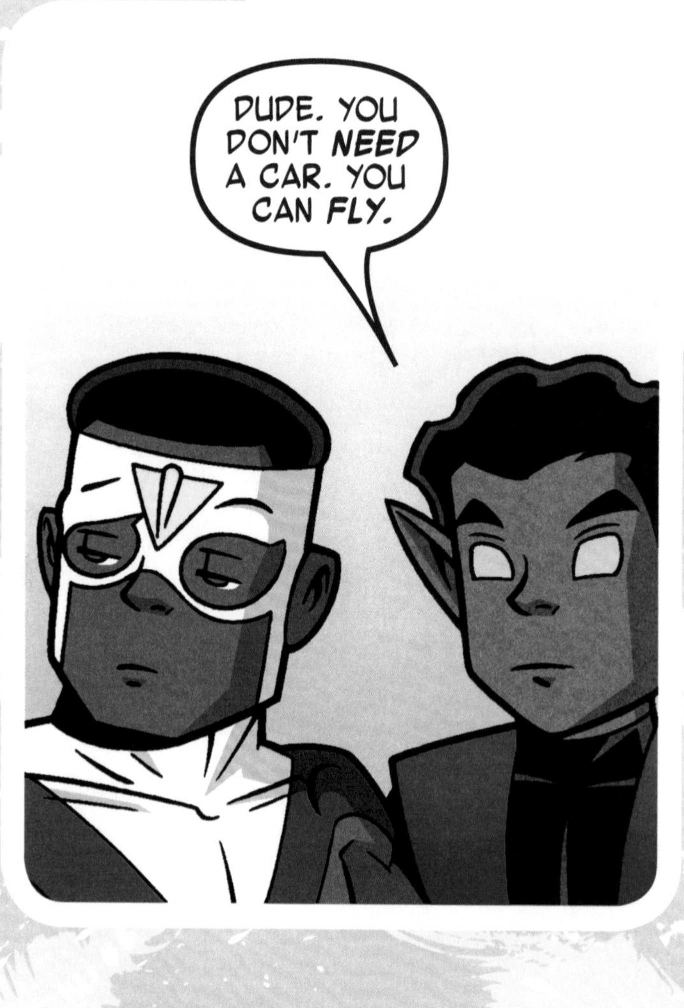
DUDE. YOU DON'T NEED A CAR. YOU CAN FLY.

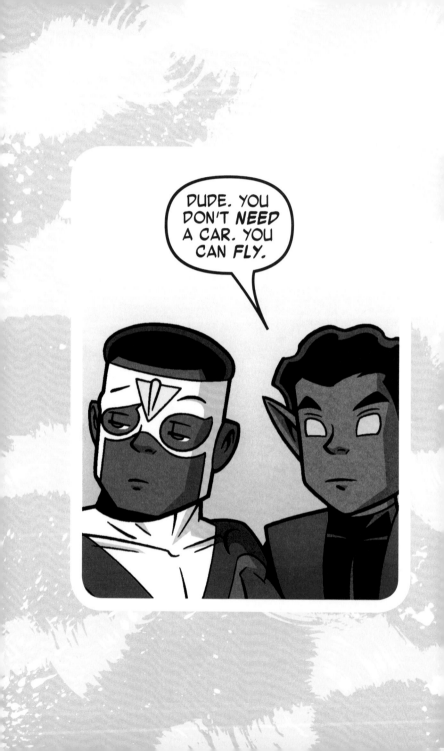

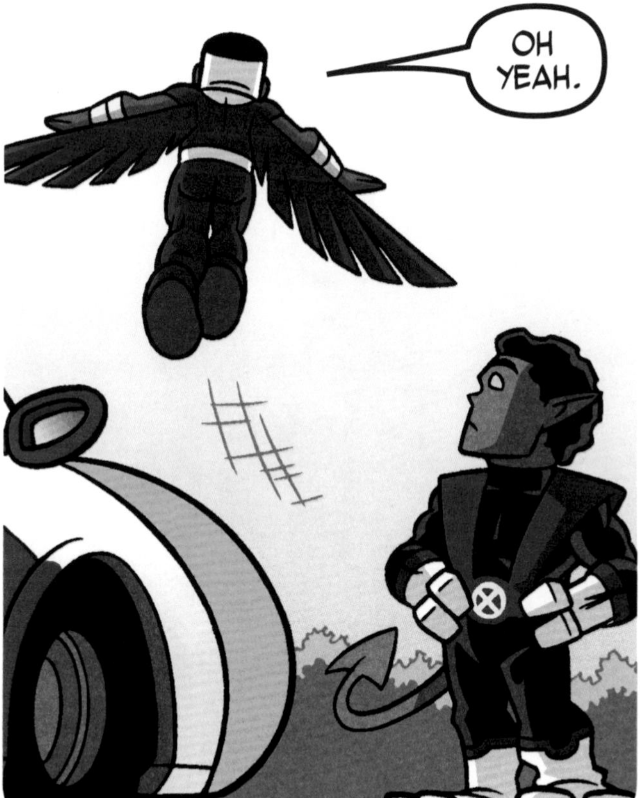
OH YEAH.

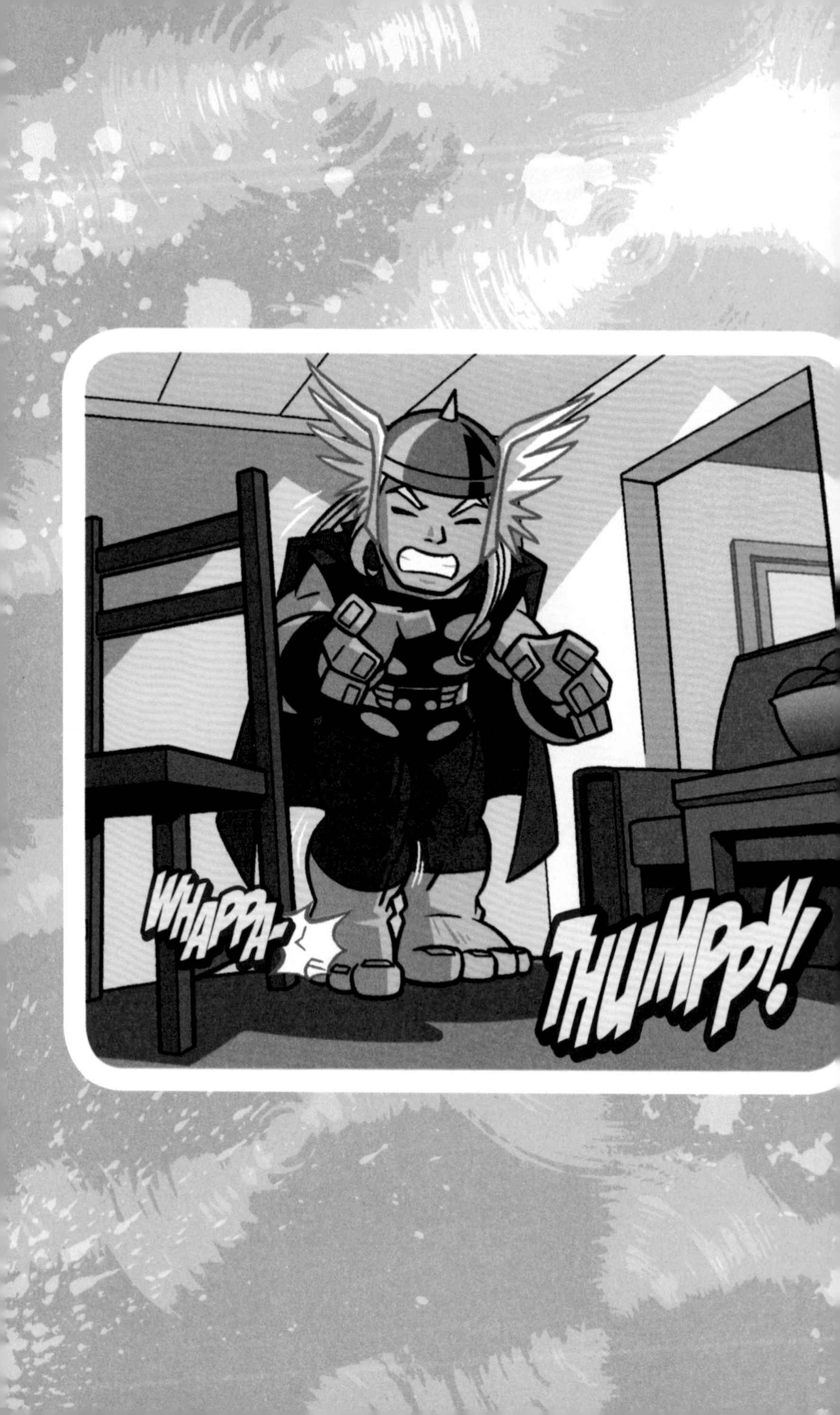
WHAPPA-
THUMPP!

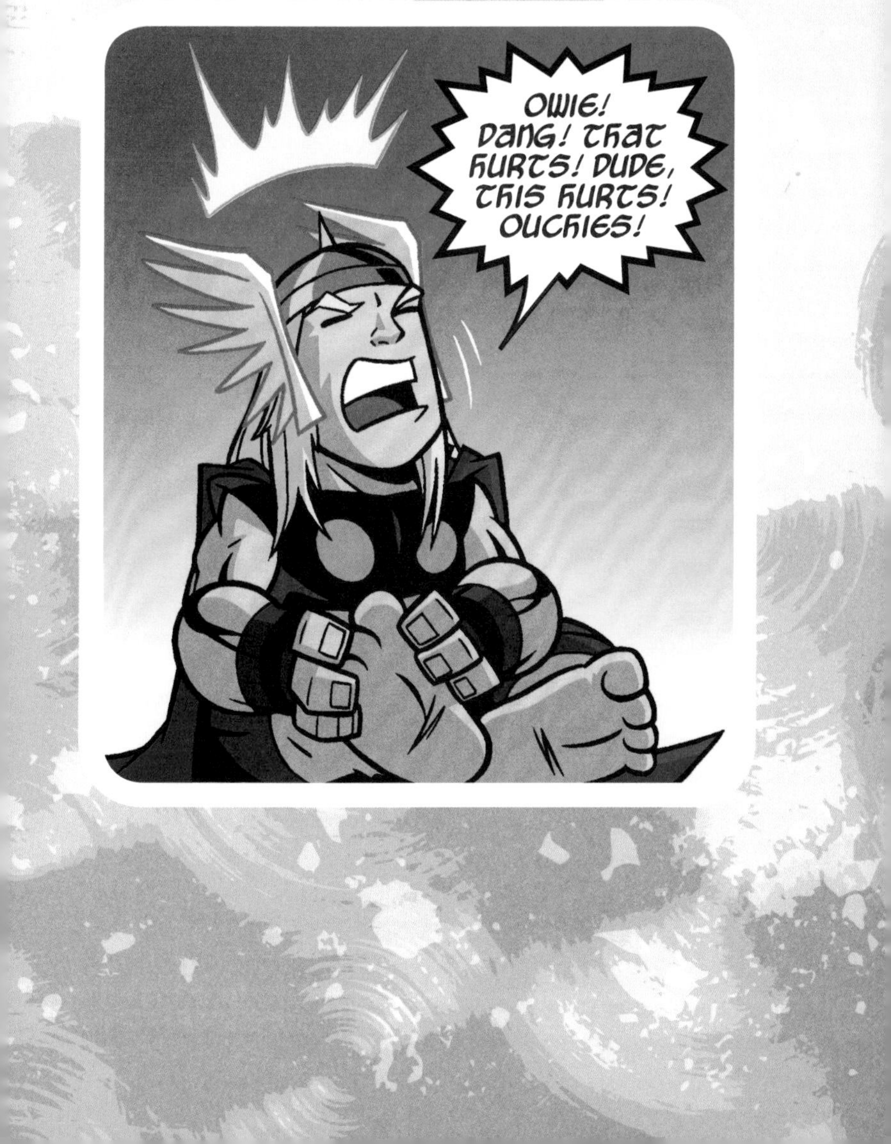
OWIE! DANG! THAT HURTS! DUDE, THIS HURTS! OUCHIES!

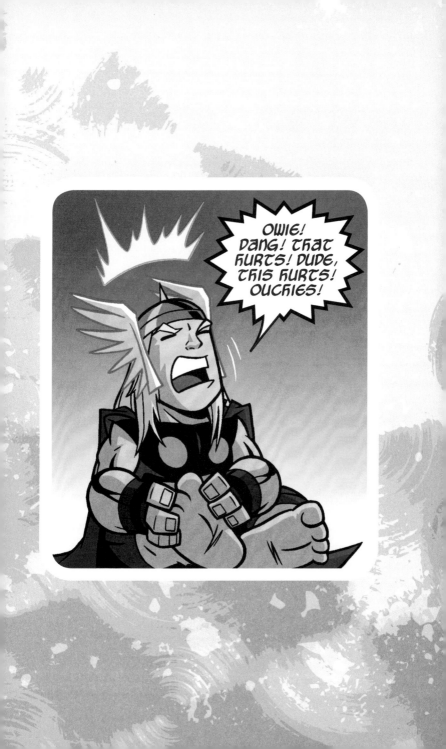

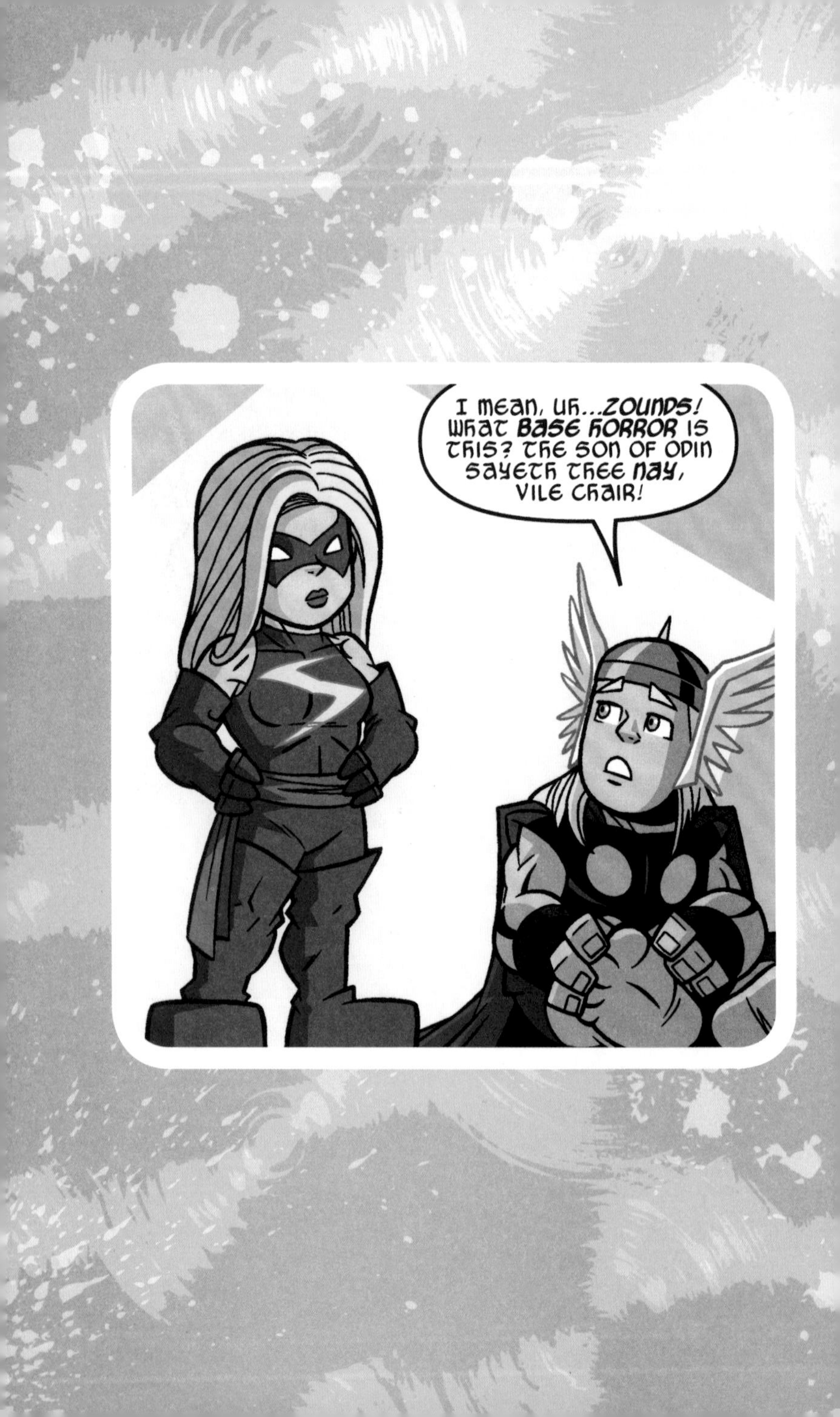
I MEAN, UH...ZOUNDS! WHAT BASE HORROR IS THIS? THE SON OF ODIN SAYETH THEE NAY, VILE CHAIR!

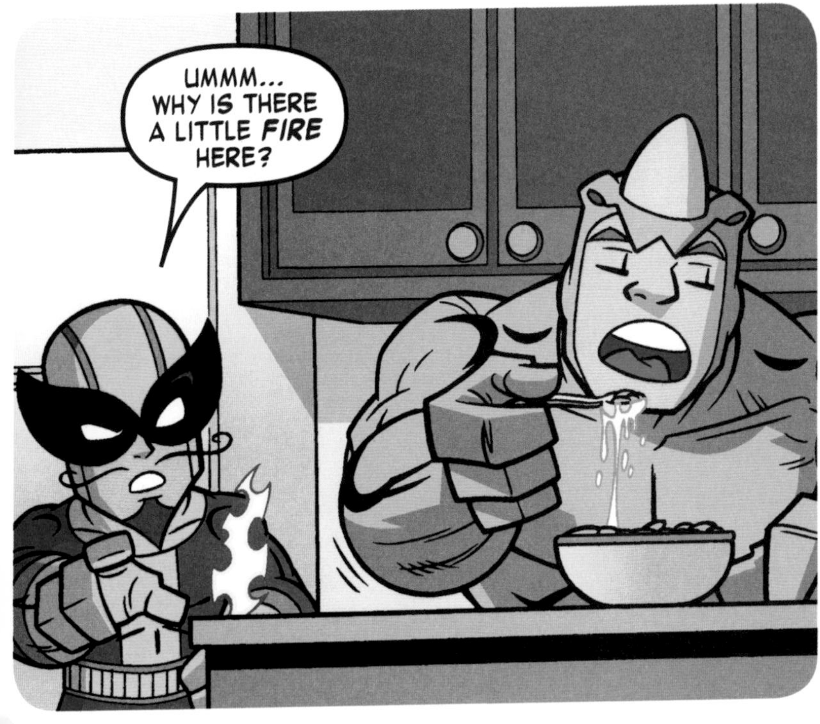
UMMM...
WHY IS THERE A LITTLE FIRE HERE?

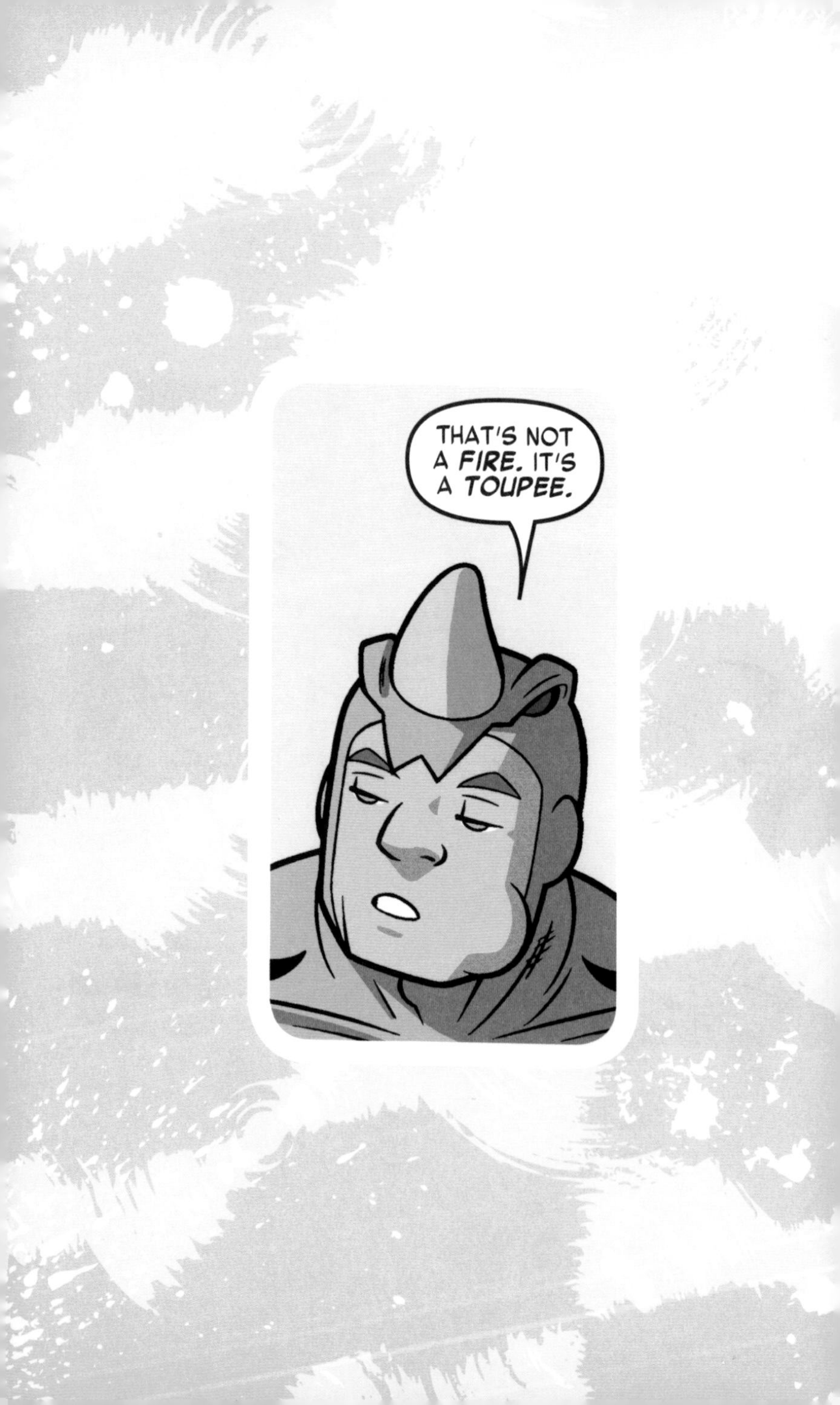
THAT'S NOT A FIRE. IT'S A TOUPEE.

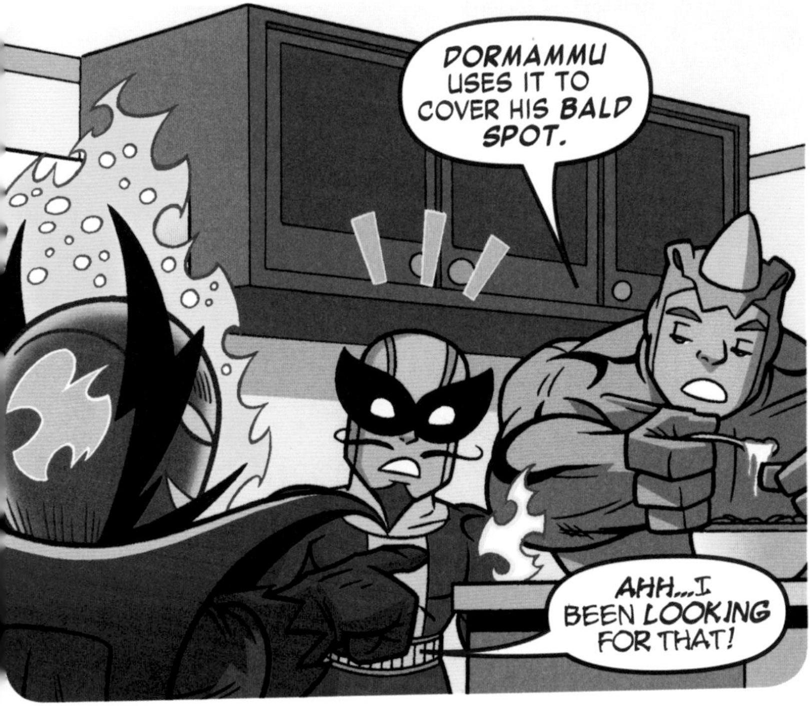
DORMAMMU USES IT TO COVER HIS BALD SPOT.
AHH...I BEEN LOOKING FOR THAT!

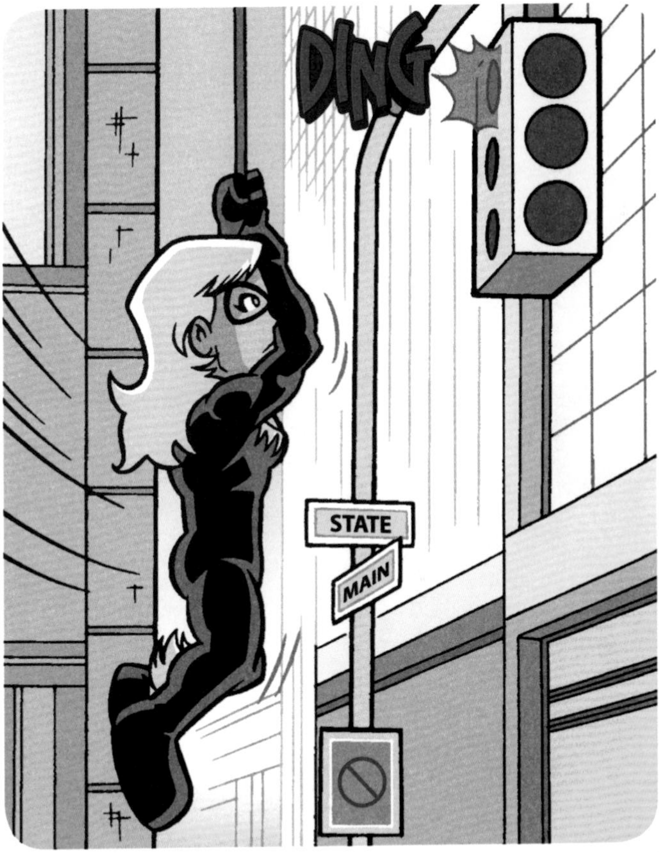
DING
STATE
MAIN

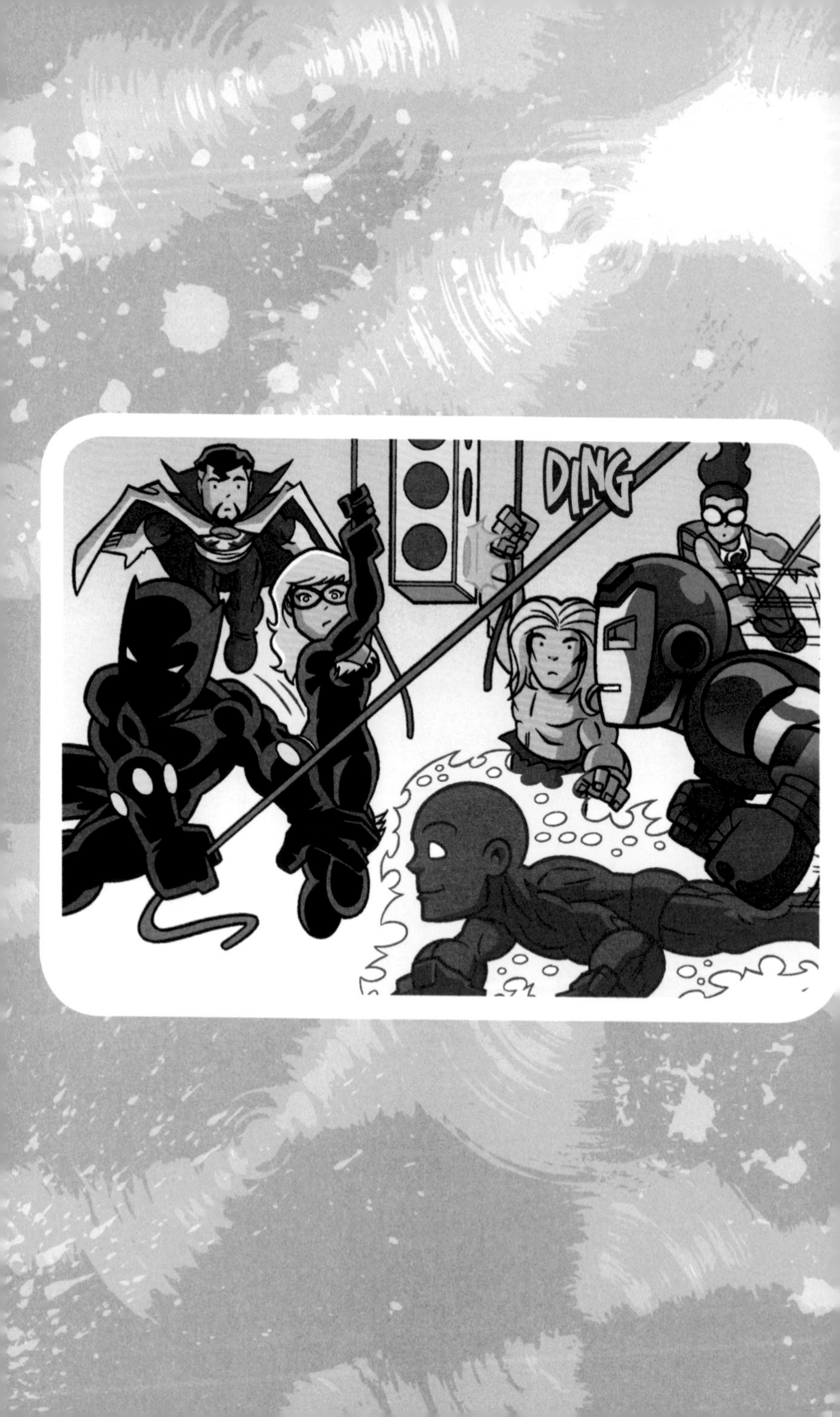
DING

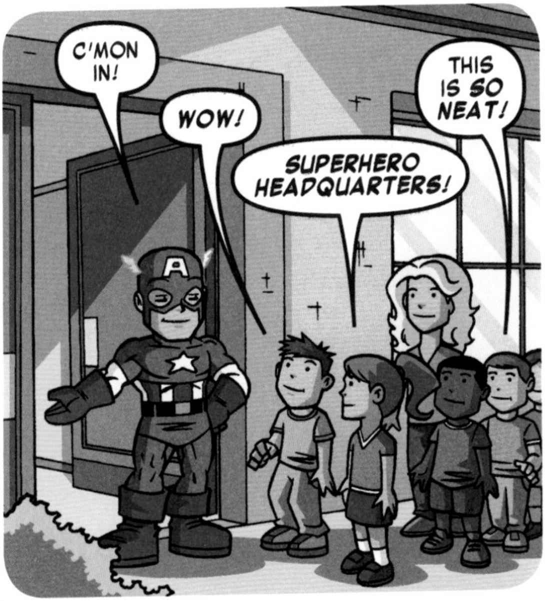
C'MON IN!
WOW!
SUPERHERO HEADQUARTERS!
THIS IS SO NEAT!

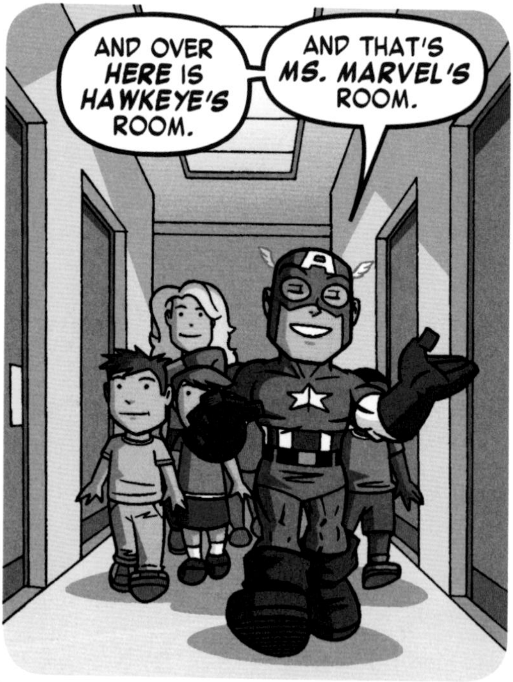
AND OVER HERE IS HAWKEYE'S ROOM.
AND THAT'S MS. MARVEL'S ROOM.

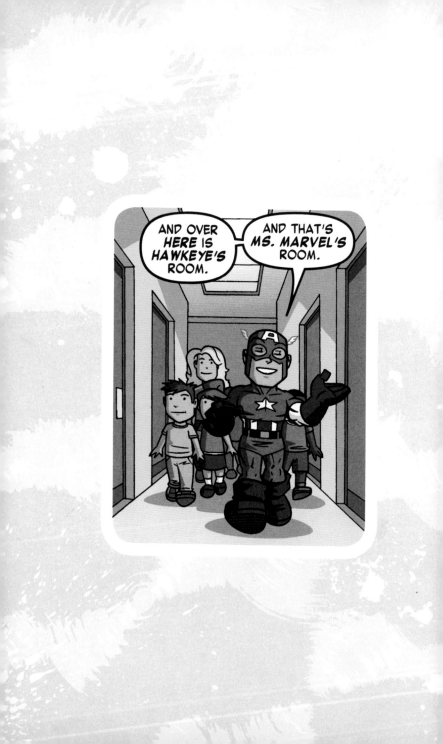

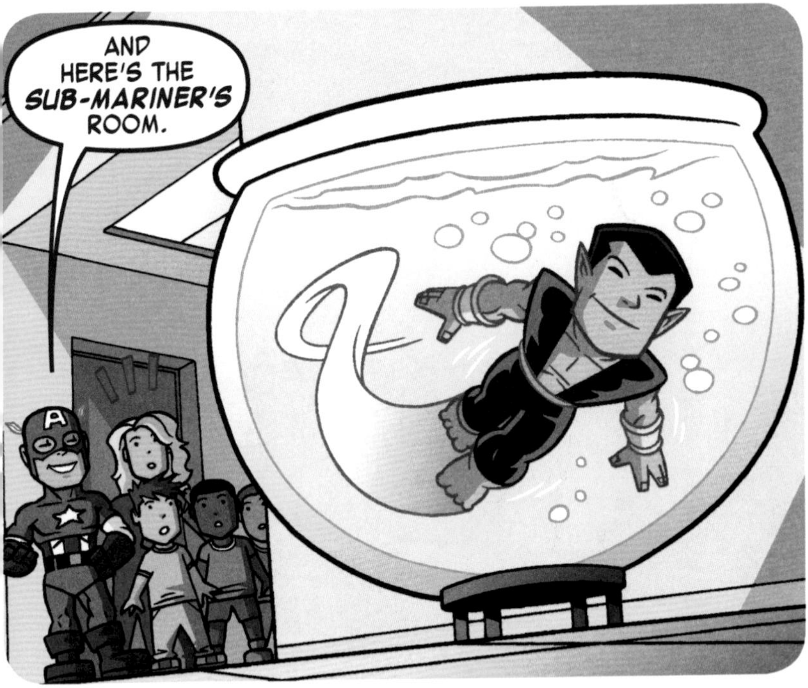
AND HERE'S THE SUB-MARINER'S ROOM.

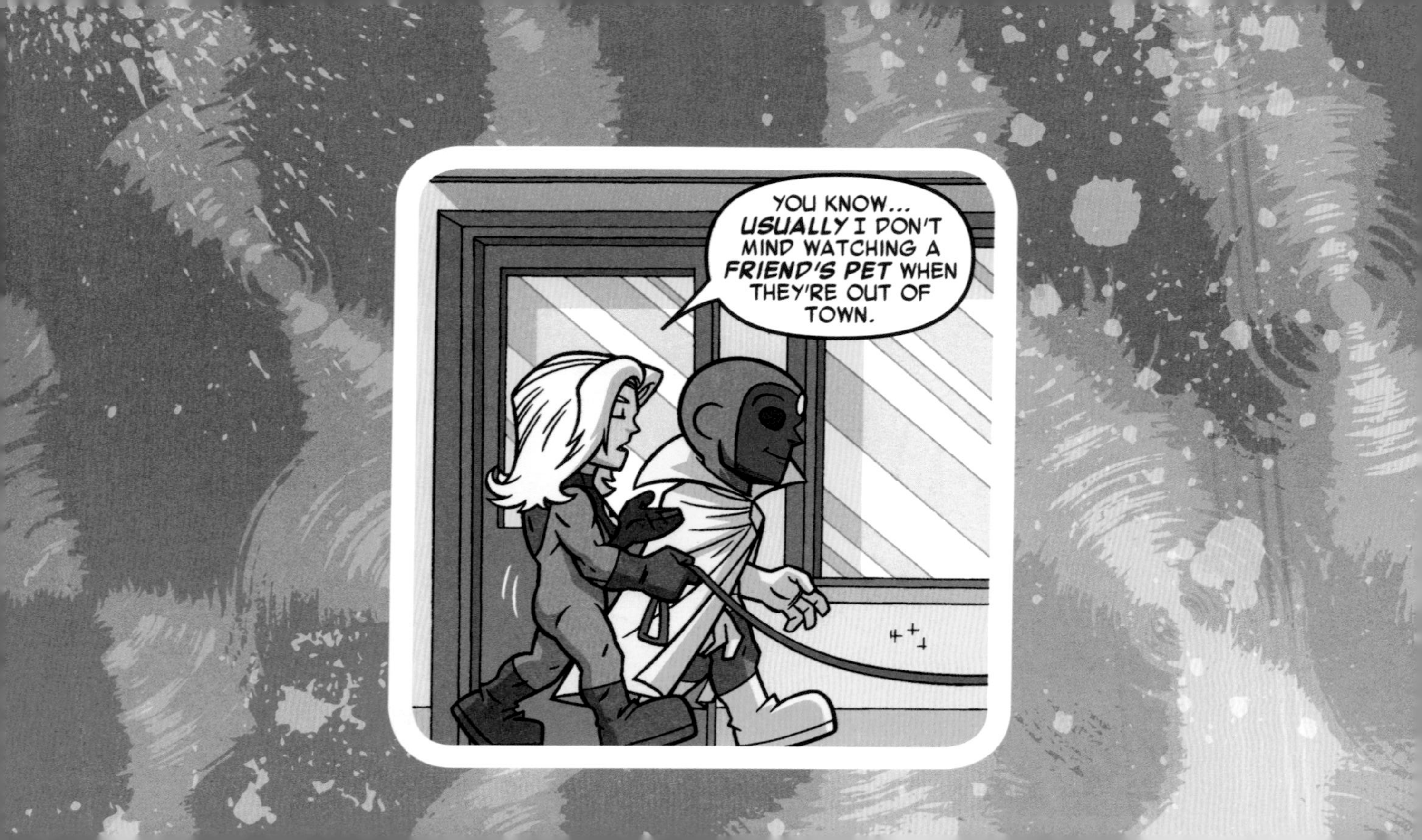
YOU KNOW... *USUALLY* I DON'T MIND WATCHING A *FRIEND'S PET* WHEN THEY'RE OUT OF TOWN.

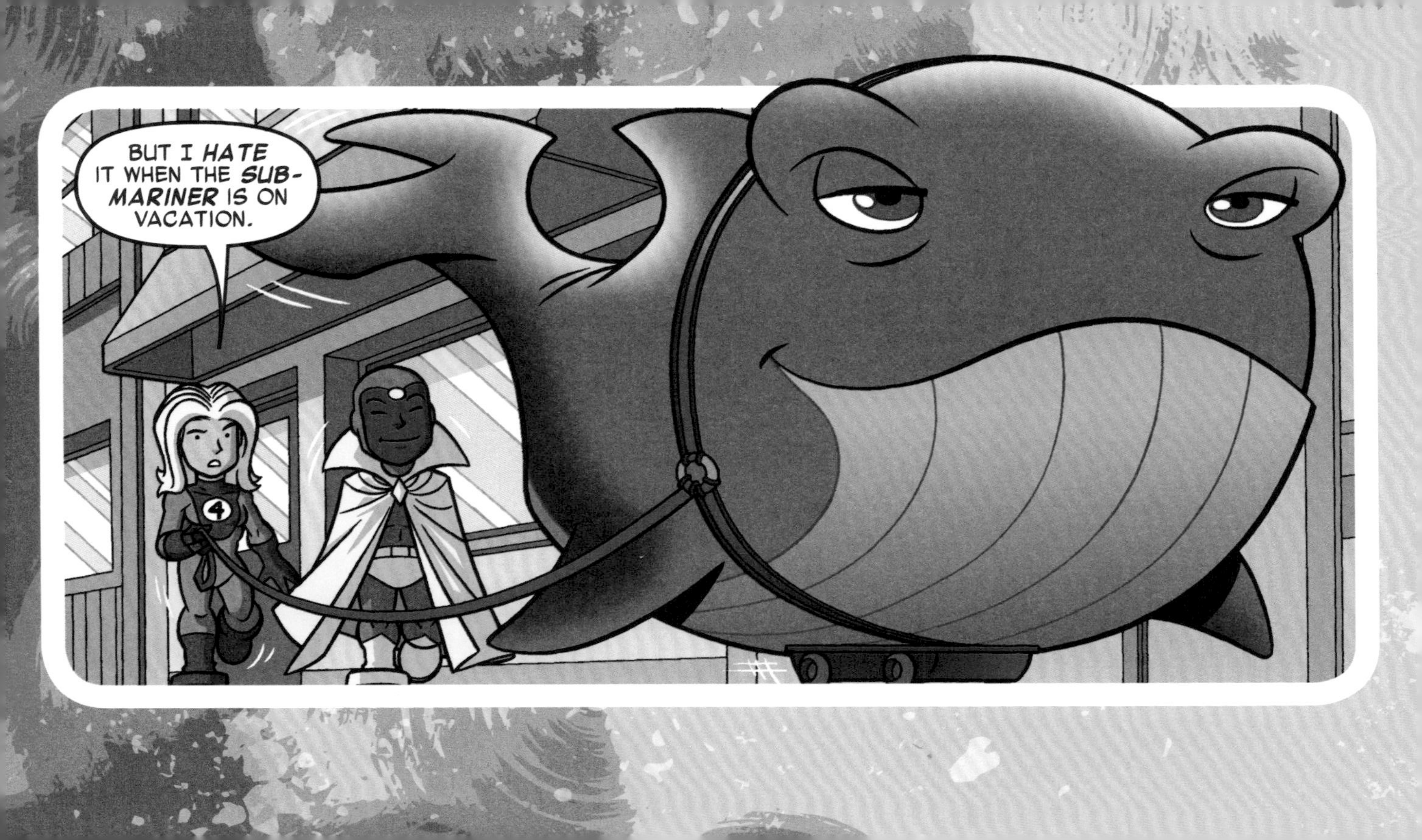
BUT I *HATE* IT WHEN THE *SUB-MARINER* IS ON VACATION.

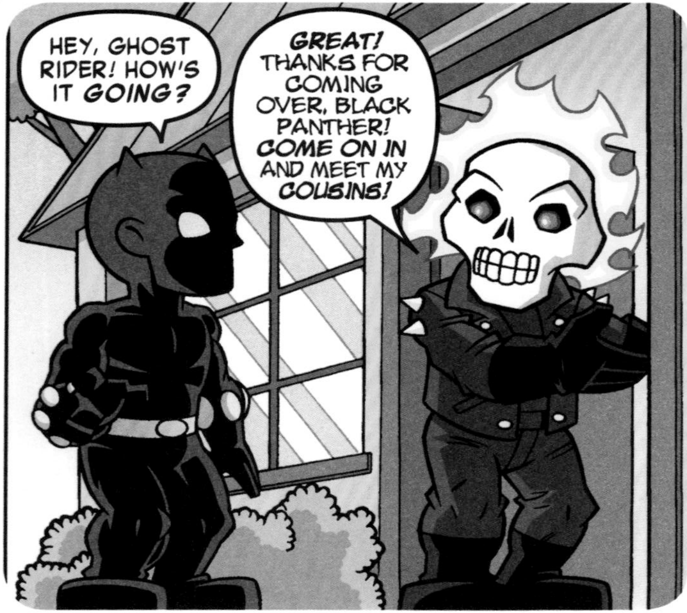
HEY, GHOST RIDER! HOW'S IT GOING?
GREAT! THANKS FOR COMING OVER, BLACK PANTHER! COME ON IN AND MEET MY COUSINS!

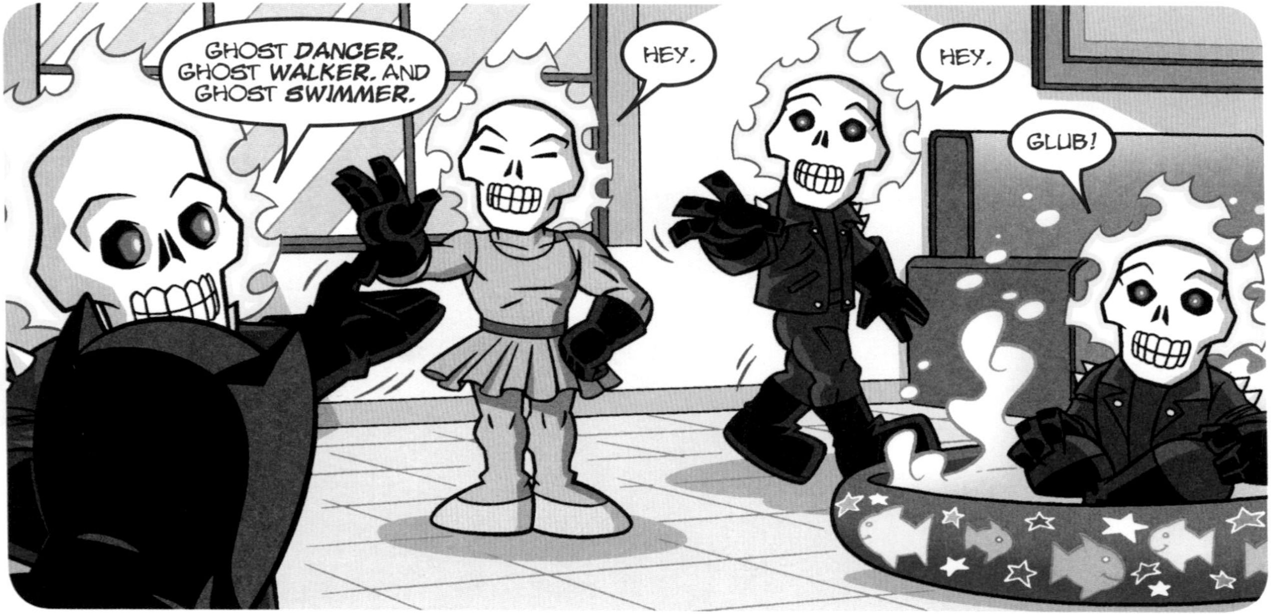
GHOST **DANCER**. GHOST **WALKER**. AND GHOST **SWIMMER**.
HEY.
HEY.
GLUB!

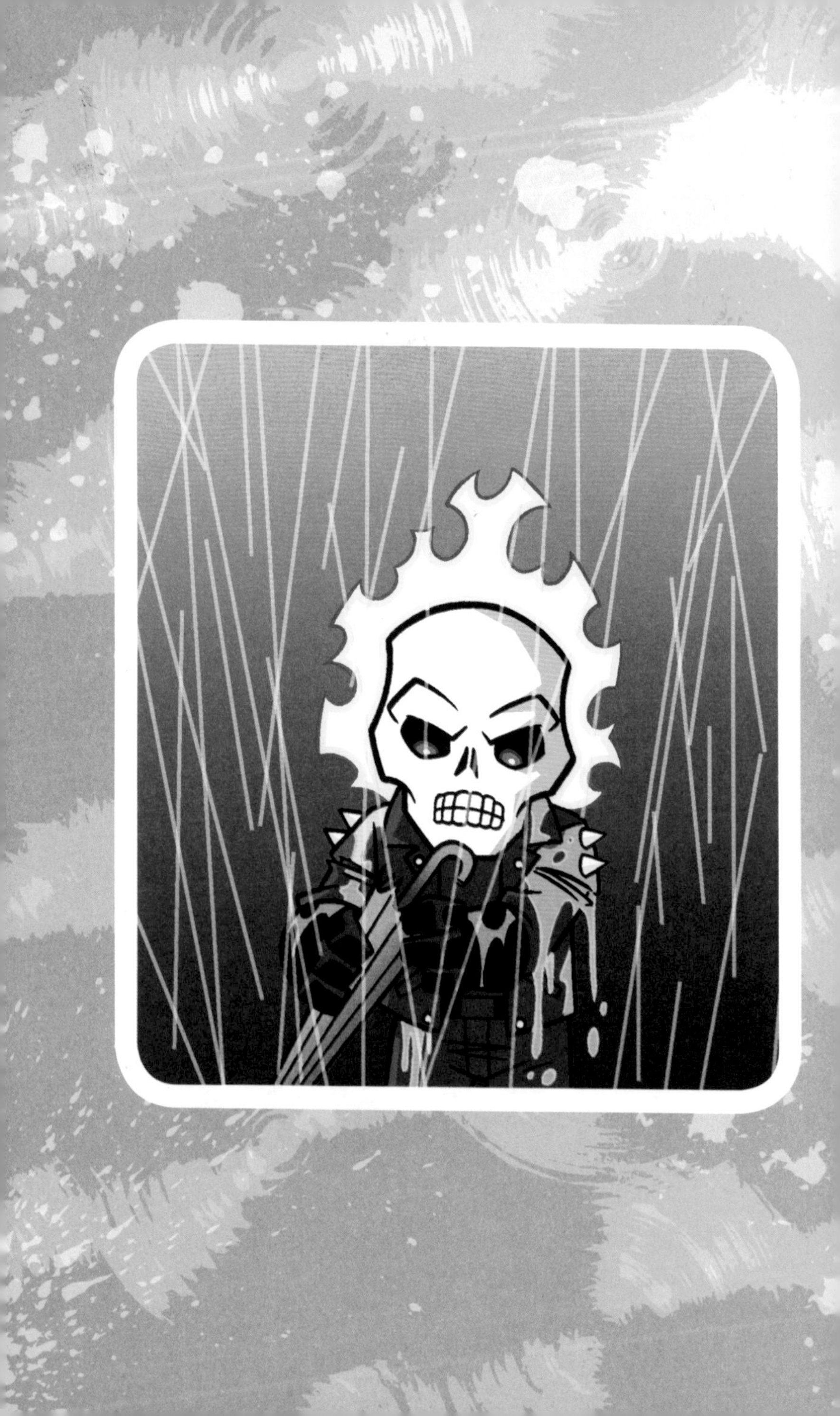

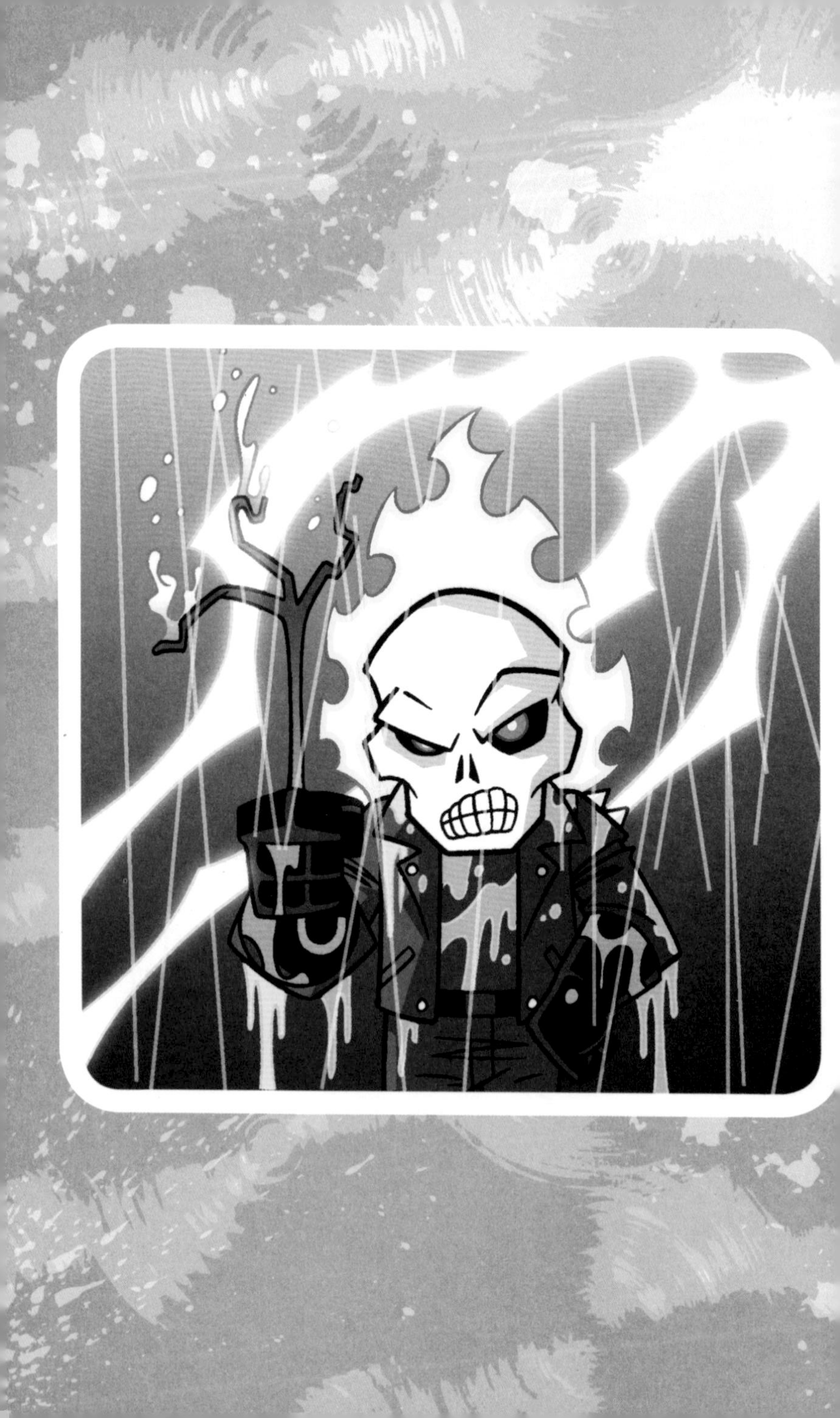

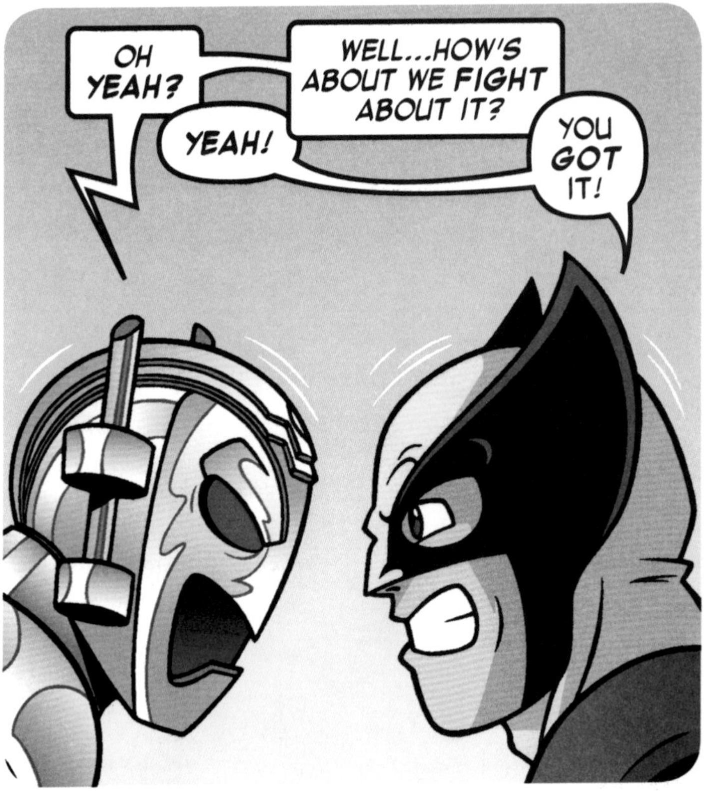
OH YEAH?
WELL...HOW'S ABOUT WE FIGHT ABOUT IT?
YEAH!
YOU GOT IT!

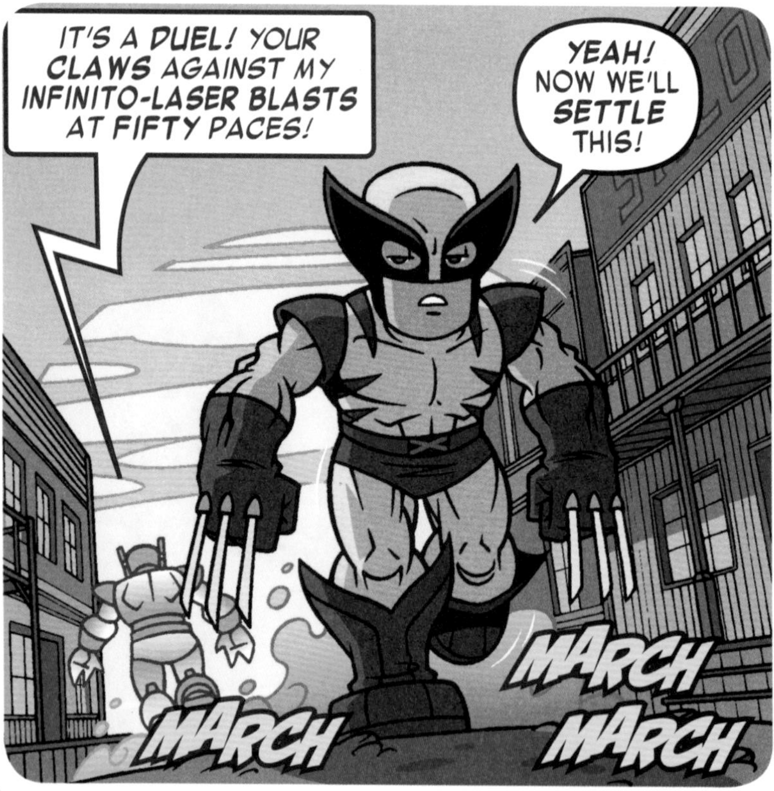
IT'S A DUEL! YOUR CLAWS AGAINST MY INFINITO-LASER BLASTS AT FIFTY PACES!
YEAH! NOW WE'LL SETTLE THIS!
MARCH
MARCH
MARCH
MARCH

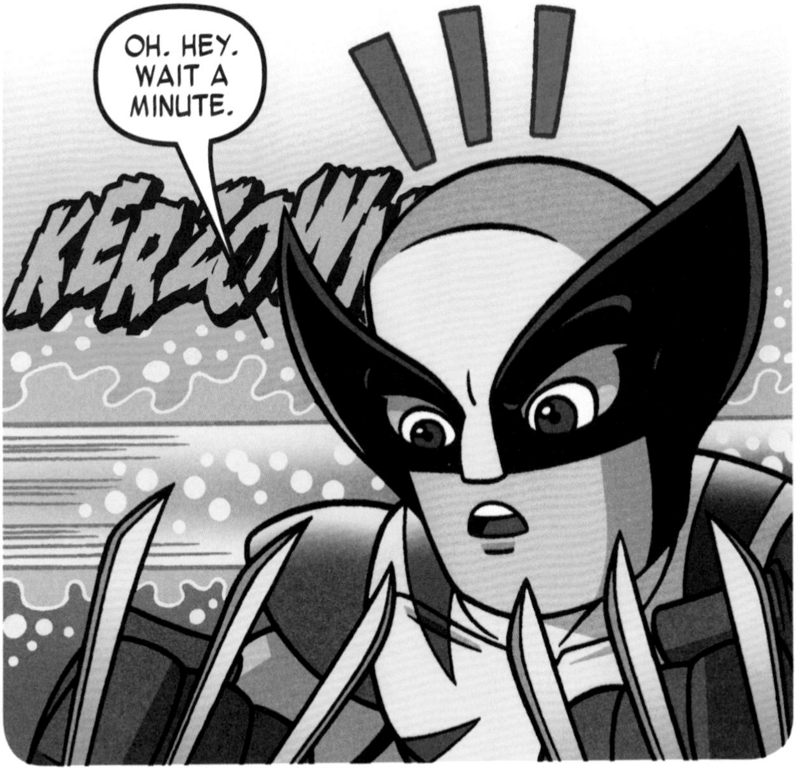
OH. HEY. WAIT A MINUTE.

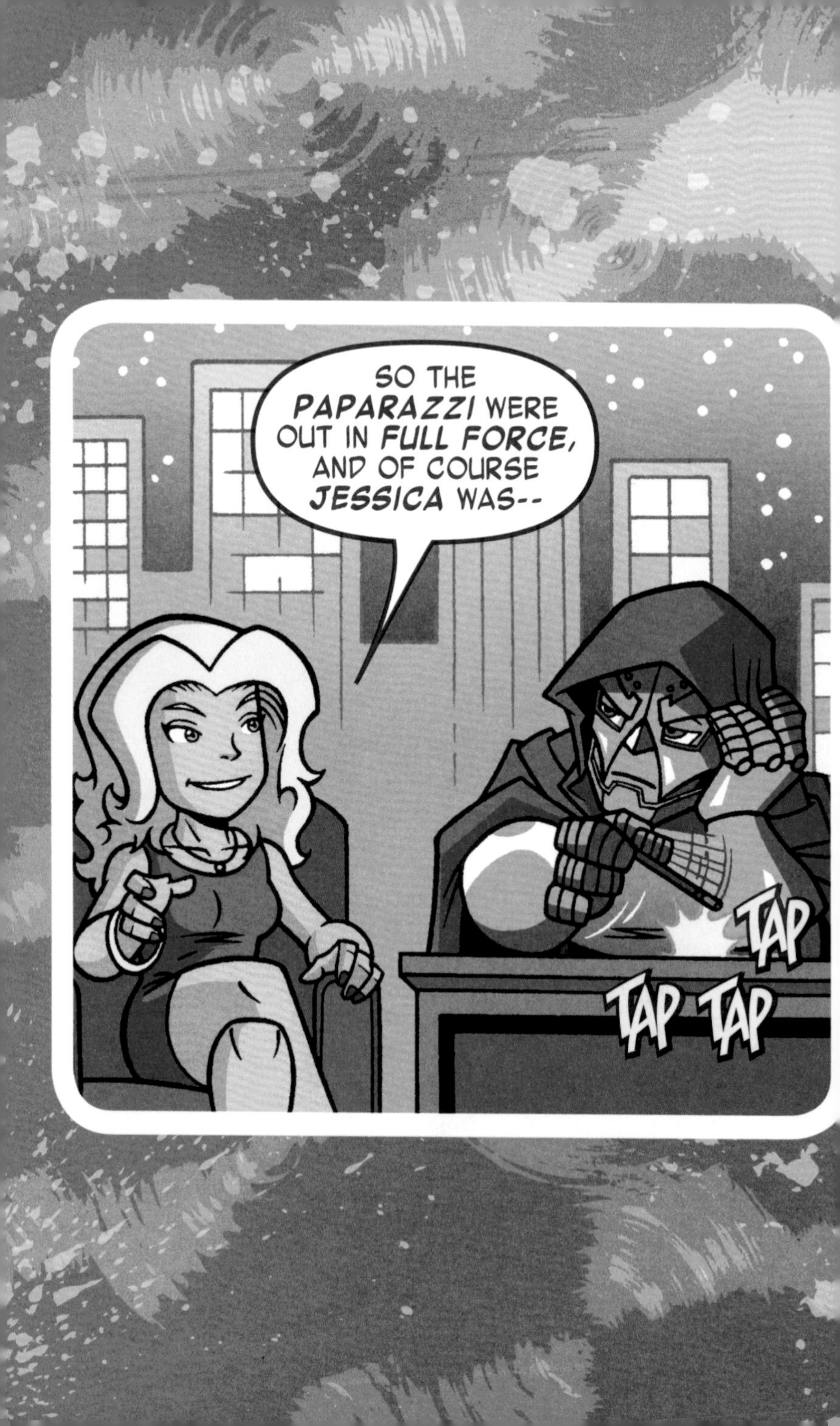
SO THE PAPARAZZI WERE OUT IN FULL FORCE, AND OF COURSE JESSICA WAS--
TAP
TAP TAP

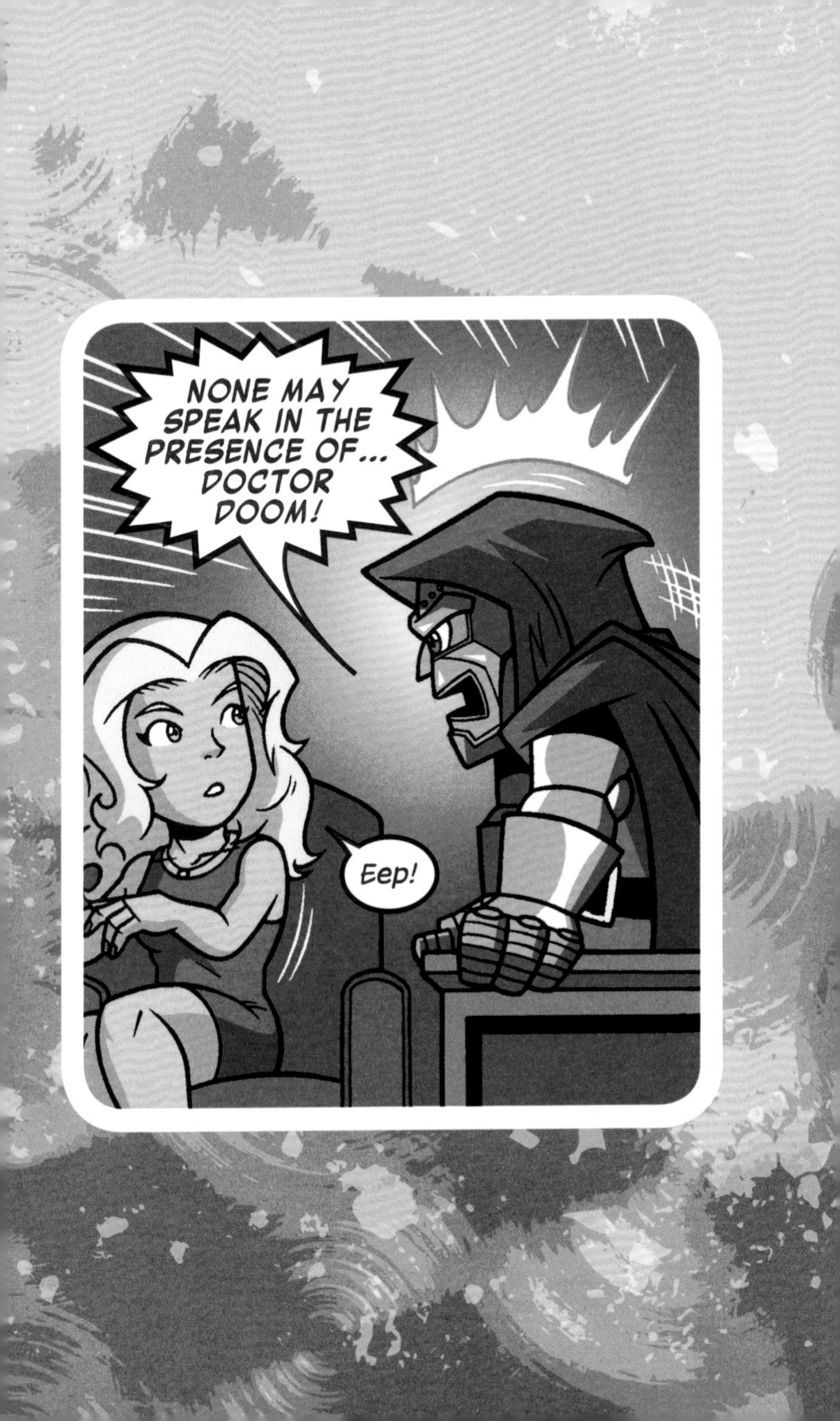
NONE MAY SPEAK IN THE PRESENCE OF... DOCTOR DOOM!
Eep!

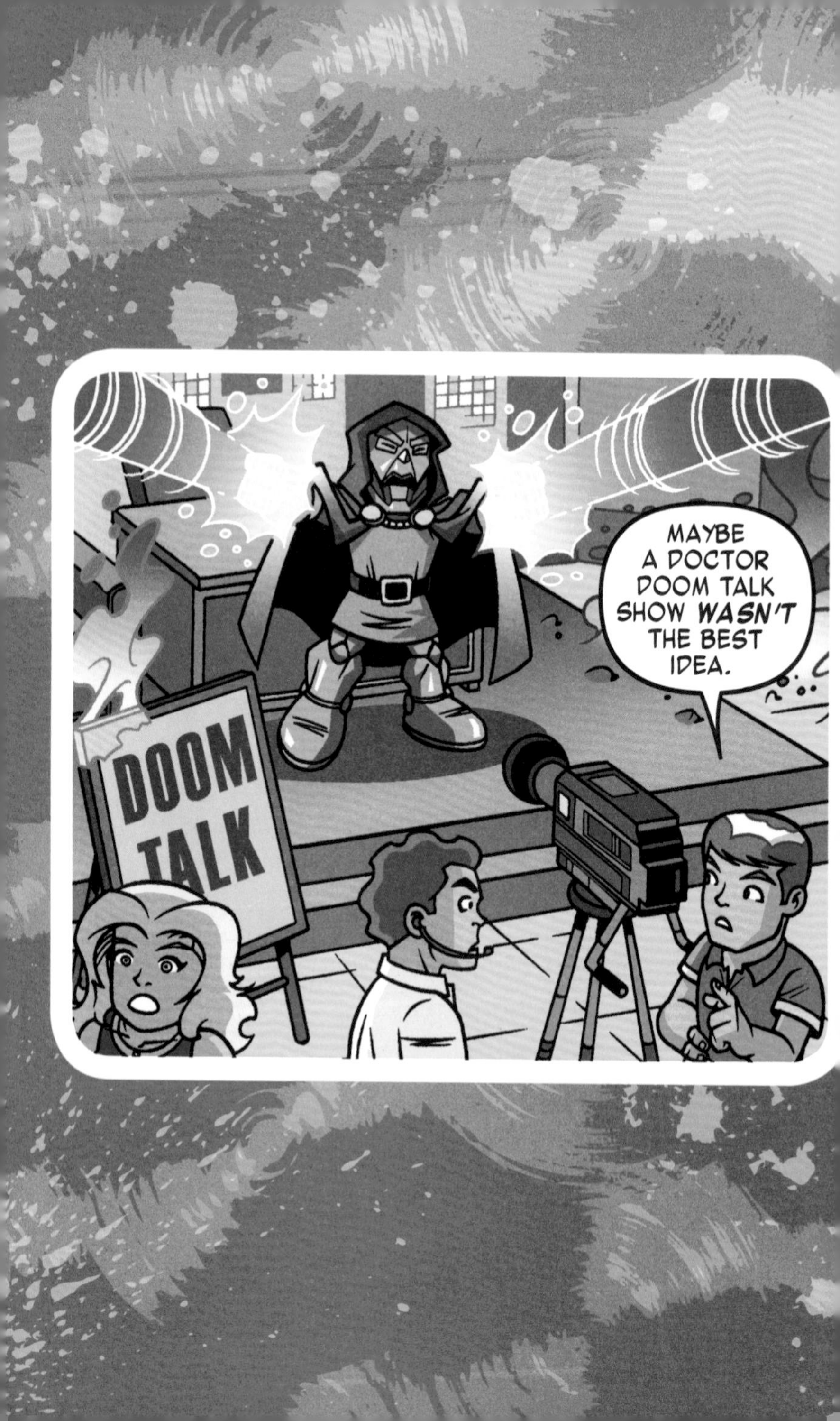
MAYBE A DOCTOR DOOM TALK SHOW WASN'T THE BEST IDEA.
DOOM TALK

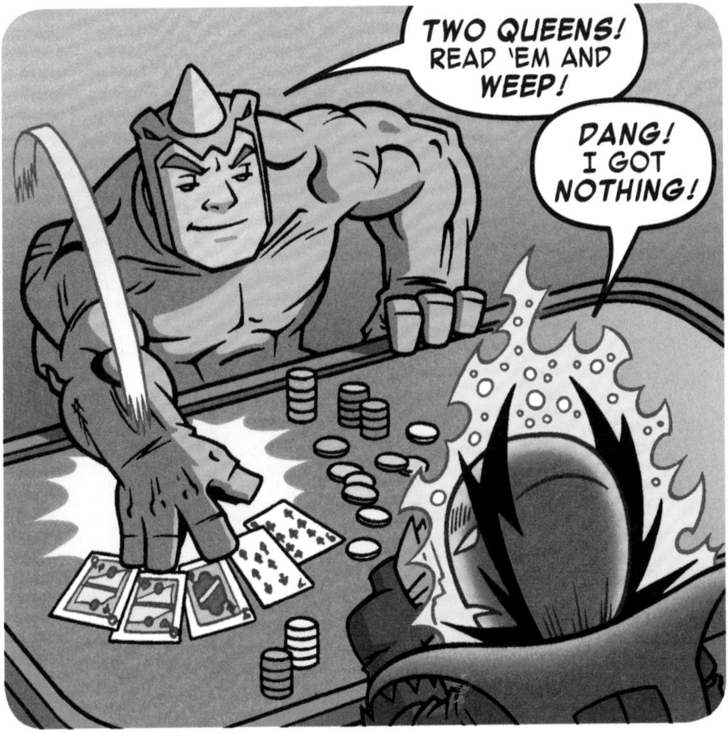
TWO QUEENS! READ 'EM AND WEEP!
DANG! I GOT NOTHING!

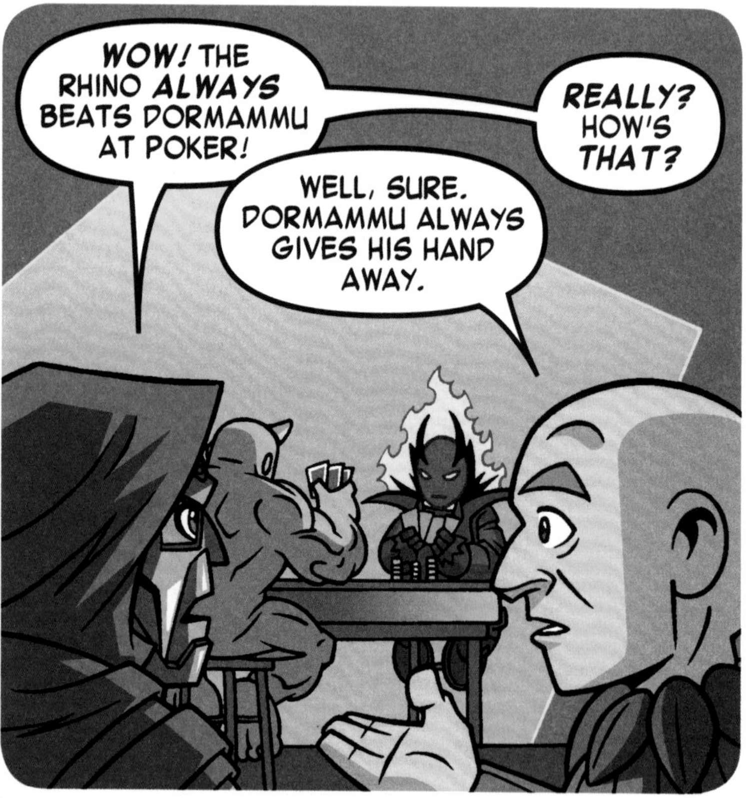
WOW! THE RHINO ALWAYS BEATS DORMAMMU AT POKER!
REALLY? HOW'S THAT?
WELL, SURE. DORMAMMU ALWAYS GIVES HIS HAND AWAY.

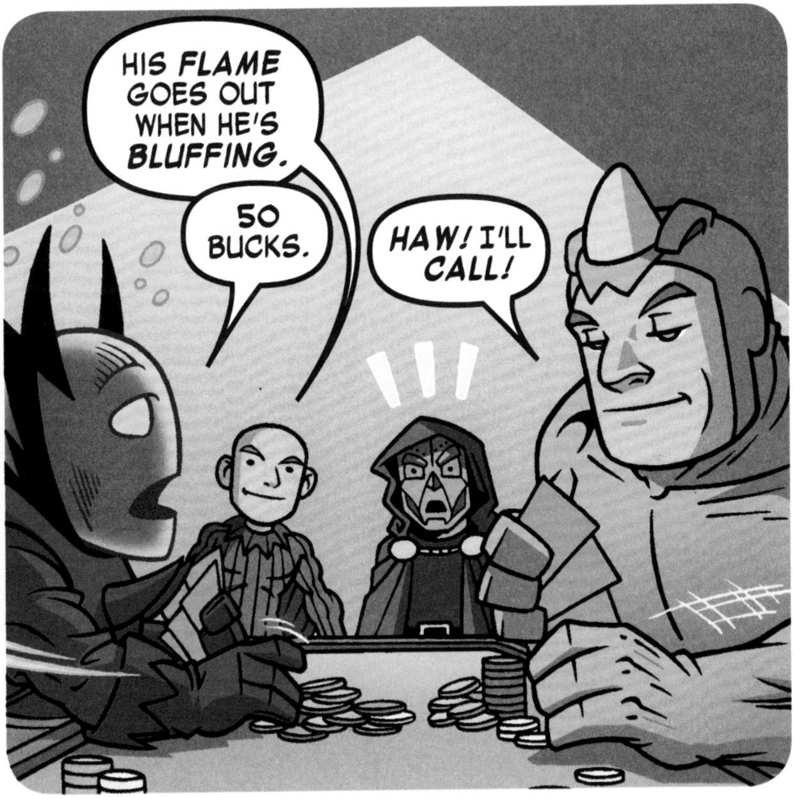
HIS FLAME GOES OUT WHEN HE'S BLUFFING.
50 BUCKS.
HAW! I'LL CALL!

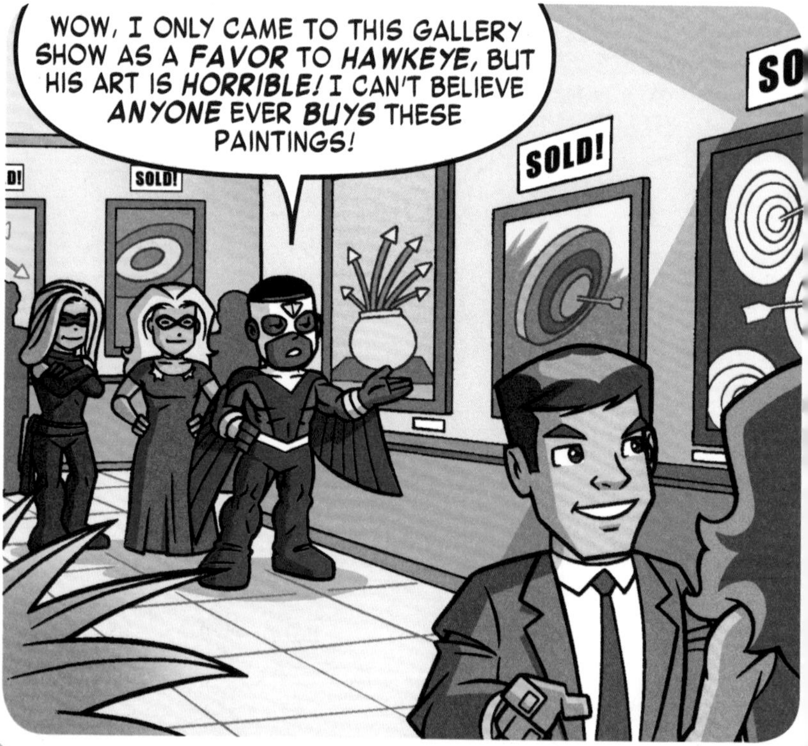
WOW, I ONLY CAME TO THIS GALLERY SHOW AS A FAVOR TO HAWKEYE, BUT HIS ART IS HORRIBLE! I CAN'T BELIEVE ANYONE EVER BUYS THESE PAINTINGS!
SOLD!
SOLD!
SOLD!

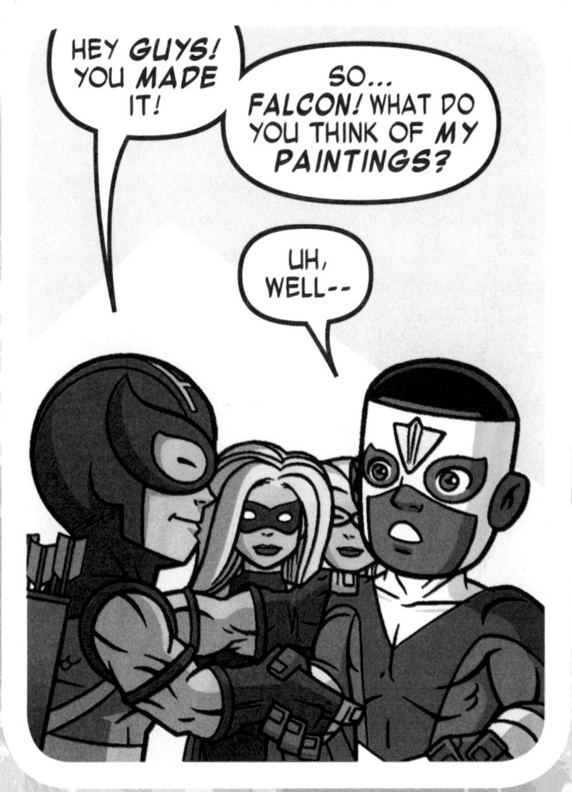
HEY GUYS! YOU MADE IT!
SO... FALCON! WHAT DO YOU THINK OF MY PAINTINGS?
UH, WELL--

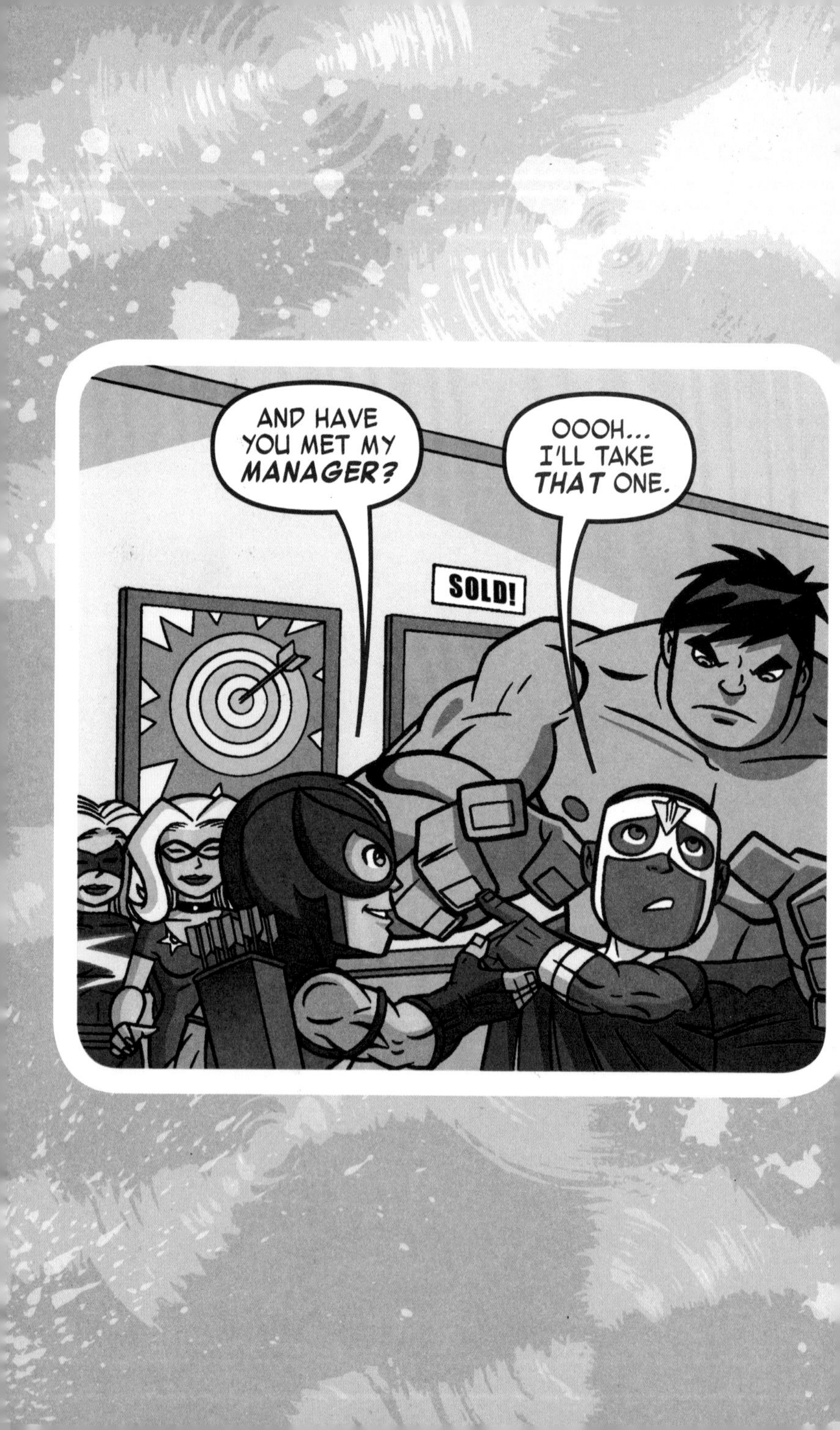
AND HAVE YOU MET MY *MANAGER*?
OOOH... I'LL TAKE *THAT* ONE.
SOLD!